DATA COLLECTION AND MAPPING

DATA COLLECTION AND MAPPING

BY
ILINA MARTIN
ADAMO JOHNSON
BASSETT MURRAY

KNOWLEDGE
BAKERS

KNOWLEDGE BAKERS

ISBN: 978-93-9001-367-8

Published by : **Knowledge Bakers**
Pune, India
Email: info@knowledgebakers.com

PREFACE

In the age of information, data serves as the lifeblood of decision-making, policy formulation, and problem-solving across various domains. From urban planning and environmental management to disaster response and market analysis, the ability to collect, analyze, and visualize data plays a pivotal role in understanding complex phenomena and guiding informed action. As we navigate the vast landscape of data collection and mapping, it becomes evident that these processes are not merely technical endeavors but integral components of a larger framework for knowledge creation and societal advancement.

This book, titled "Data Collection and Mapping," emerges as a comprehensive guide to understanding the principles, methodologies, and applications of data collection and mapping techniques. Through collaboration with experts and practitioners in the field, we aim to provide readers with a nuanced understanding of the processes involved in gathering, processing, and representing spatial and non-spatial data.

As editors of this volume, we have curated a collection of chapters that cover a wide range of topics within data collection and mapping, including survey design, data acquisition methods, spatial analysis techniques, visualization tools, and quality assurance practices. Each chapter offers insights from both theoretical and practical perspectives, drawing on real-world examples, case studies, and best practices to illustrate the complexities of data collection and mapping processes.

Furthermore, this book seeks to highlight the interdisciplinary nature of data collection and mapping and its applications in diverse fields such as geography, environmental science, public health, transportation, and urban planning. By showcasing innovative approaches, emerging technologies, and ethical considerations, we aim to inspire readers to adopt a holistic approach to data collection and mapping, fostering collaboration and knowledge exchange across disciplines and sectors.

As we embark on this journey of exploration and discovery in the realm of data collection and mapping, we extend our gratitude to the contributors whose expertise and dedication have enriched this volume. We hope that "Data Collection and Mapping" serves as a valuable resource for students, researchers, professionals, and policymakers alike, empowering them to harness the power of data to address complex challenges and drive positive change in their communities and beyond.

Ilina Martin

Adamo Johnson

Bassett Murray

CONTENTS

CHAPTER- 1

SPATIAL DATA MODELS AND THE PUBLIC DOMAIN

In this lesson, we:

- ☆ Review typical spatial data models in the context of geographic information systems (GIS) today
- ☆ Dig into raster and vector data models, format, and quality
- ☆ Introduce public domain spatial data
- ☆ Review scale, coordinate systems, and projections.

Lesson Topics

This introductory lesson covers three topics and takes approximately 50 minutes to complete. We recommend working through each topic in the order in which they are listed below.

- ☆ Spatial Data Models
- ☆ Digging into Raster and Vector Data
- ☆ Spatial Data in the Public Domain
- ☆ Review of Coordinate Systems

1. SPATIAL DATA MODELS

GIS Applications

Let us briefly review some common applications of GIS in conservation and natural resources management. With spatial data and GIS, we can ask questions and solve problems such as the following:

Image © Shutterstock, Inc.

Finding locations (where is X?)

- ☆ Finding entities at certain locations (what is at location Y?)
- ☆ Examining spatial relationships (why is object X located at location Y?)
- ☆ Finding best routes
- ☆ Finding most suitable sites
- ☆ Predicting future change
- ☆ Analyzing land cover/use conversions
- ☆ Looking at questions of environmental justice
- ☆ Analyzing policy outcomes

GIS technology integrates spatial information from many sources to answer a multitude of questions.

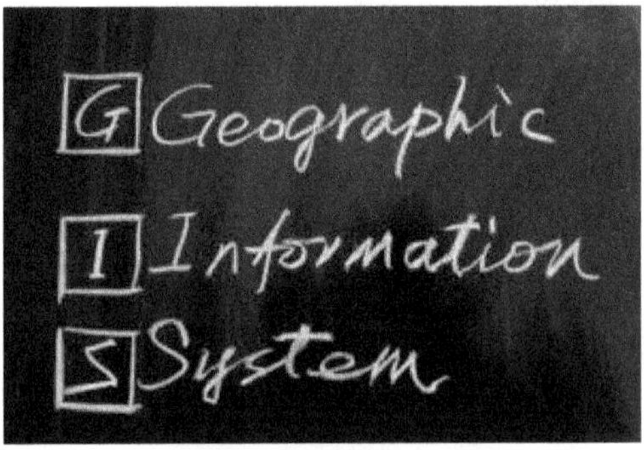

Image © Shutterstock, Inc.

Four Key Parts of GIS

Geographic or spatial data are just one piece of a GIS. Together the system includes the following:

- ☆ Places with locational information, or spatial data (a depiction or model of the real world)
- ☆ A way to organize attributes of the spatial data, or database (such as Arc Catalog)
- ☆ Tools to manipulate and analyze spatial data, or geoprocessing functions (such as ArcToolBox)
- ☆ An interface, so we can make these pieces work together (e.g., QGIS, ArcMap, ArcGIS Pro, or ArcGIS online)

Geographic data are composed of two components, both of which are stored in GIS layers:

- ☆ **Spatial Data** refer to the points, lines, and polygons, or raster cells, which represent features on earth (georeferenced to real-world coordinates). Spatial data can be represented using various **spatial data models**, which are described further in this lesson.

- ☆ This badger den could be mapped as a point feature. *Image © Shutterstock, Inc.*
- ☆ **Attribute Data** consist of characteristics or properties that describe spatial entities.

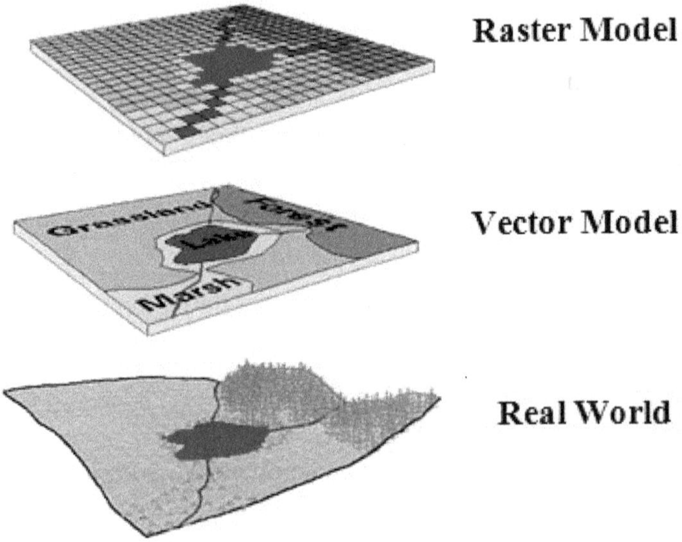

Image source: http://mwiki.gichd.org/IM/Types_of_Data

Geographic data models are the various geometric structures for storing geographic spatial data.We use different kinds of data models to:

☆ Define the classes of objects that can be represented and how they behave or act within GIS

☆ Define the basic design pattern for depicting the real world and how it is abstracted in GIS

☆ Common data models include:

- Raster
- Vector
- TIN (triangulated irregular network)

Geographic Data Models

Raster Data Models represent spatial data as a matrix or a grid of georeferenced cells (pixels) generated by a regularly spaced sampling of phenomena. They are either discrete (thematic—like land cover classes) or continuous (like soil moisture) and provide wall-to-wall coverage in a data layer.

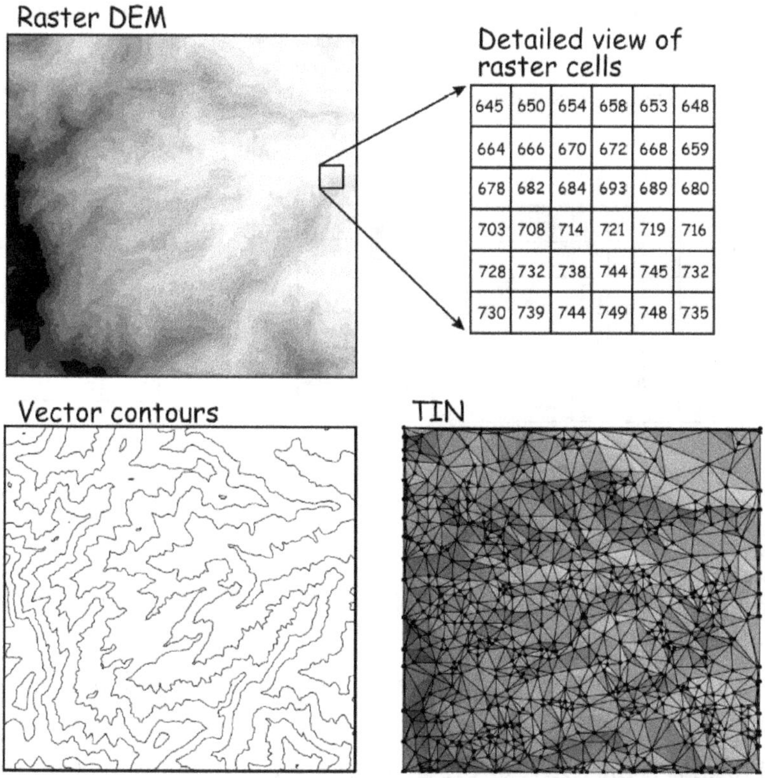

Fig 2-42, Image

Sou rce: Bostad www.paulbolstad.net/gisbook.html

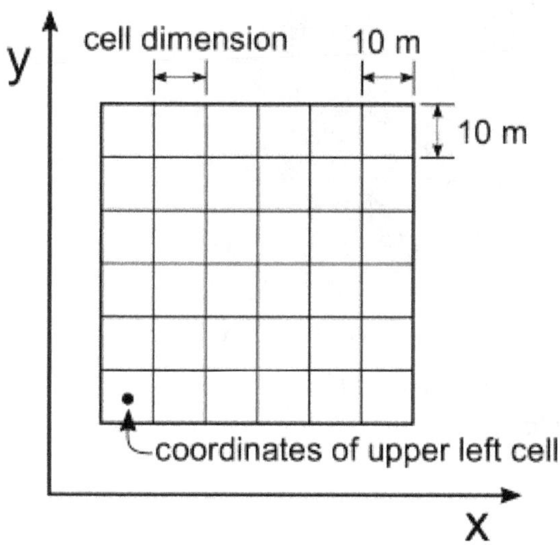

Graphic showing X and Y coordinates of raster data. *Illustration drawn by Ashley Kissick, 2018*

Pixel or cell size, or resolution, is important for display, analysis, and operations.

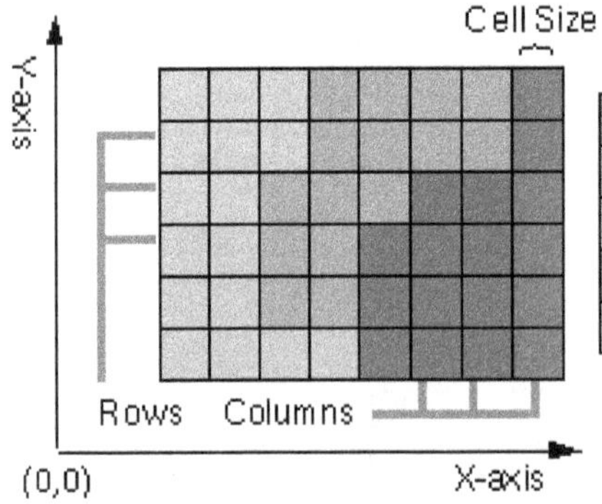

Value Attribute Table (VAT)

Value	Count	Soil	Suit.
1	11	Water	0
2	15	Id3	1
3	8	Sg	3
4	6	Id2	1
5	8	Tn4	2

Graphic of raster cells and values.

Image source: http://help.arcgis.com/en/geodatabase/10.0/sdk/arcsde/concepts/raster/entities/rasters_attr.htm

Raster data can be stored in a variety of formats, with grid and image formats being the most common.

Grid format is the native or proprietary raster format used by ESRI software to represent discrete and continuous raster data.

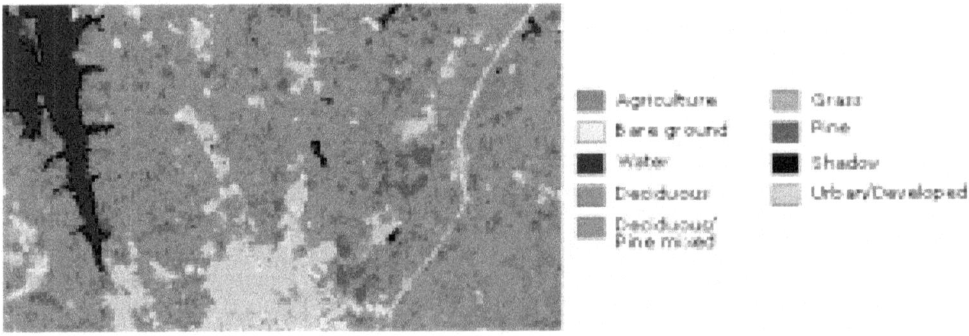

Thematic raster data.

Source: http://desktop.arcgis.com/en/arcmap/10.3/manage-data/raster-and-images/what-is-raster-data.htm.

Example of continuous raster data.

Source: http://desktop.arcgis.com/en/arcmap/10.3/manage-data/raster-and-images/what-is-raster-data.htm.

Image format collectively means raster data with cells that store brightness values and can be derived from aerial photos, satellite imagery, and scanned maps. The raster images below illustrate an aerial photo, and a scanned topographic quadrangle map.

Aerial Photo. © Shutterstock, Inc.

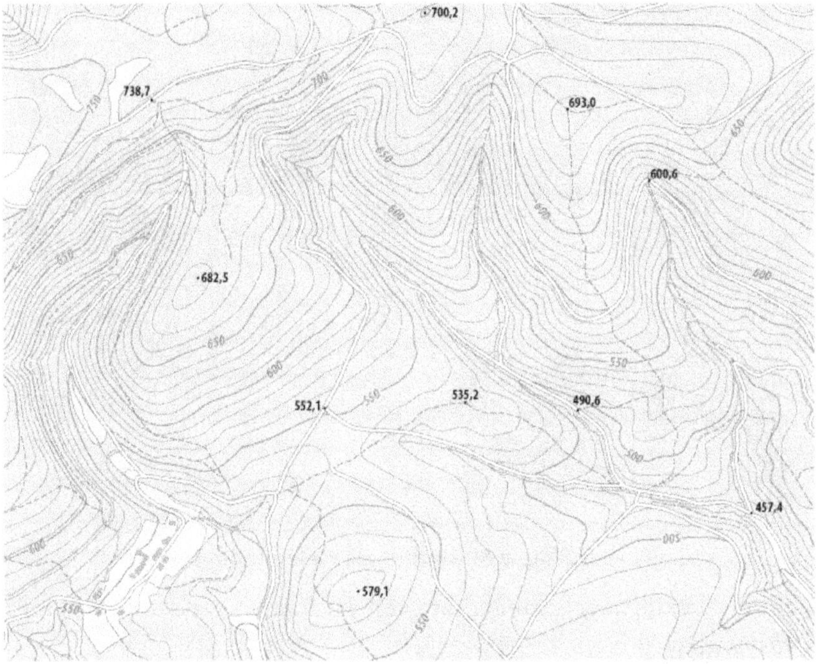

Scanned Topographic Quadrangle Map. © Shutterstock, Inc.

Raster Data Examples and Applications

Raster data are commonly used for themes that cover the whole map area, such as elevation, temperature, and precipitation. Examples include the following:

Climate and Ocean Data

Land Cover

Satellite Imagery

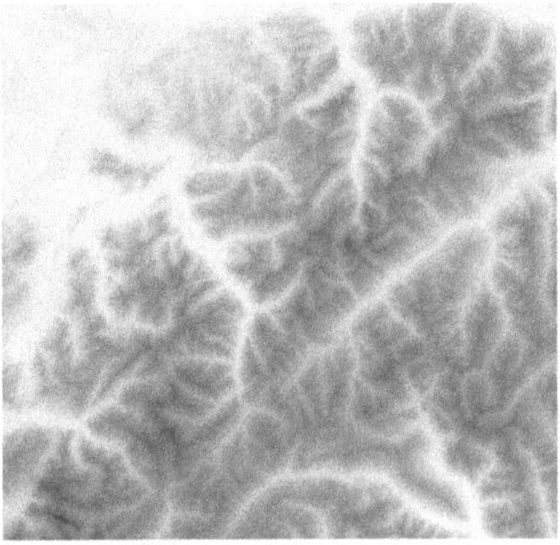

DEMs (Digital Elevation Models)

Weather Data

Images © Shutterstock, Inc.

These data are widely applied in:

☆ Environmental science

☆ Change detection

☆ Modeling

Vector

The vector data model displays spatial data as *points*, *lines*, and *polygons*, and each entity is georeferenced.

Points represent objects by a single X,Y coordinate pair.

Lines are composed of line segments connected by vertices (nodes) and are defined by the coordinate pairs of the nodes.

Polygons have a perimeter defined by line segments where the start and end node share the same geographic coordinates.

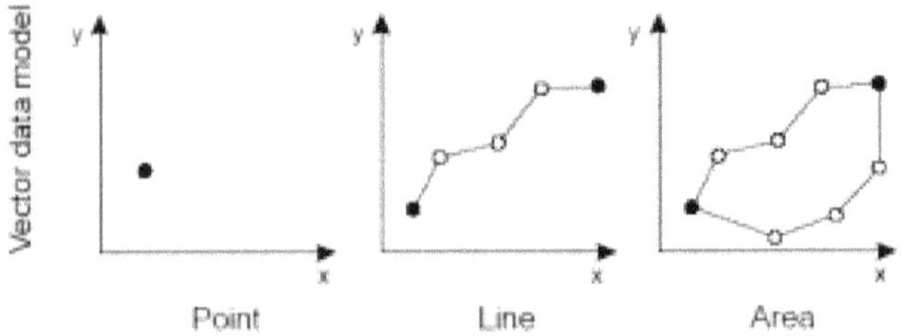

Illustration of vector data.

Source: http://www.catalonia.org/cartografia/Clase_03/Raster_Vector.html

Each object represented in vector format has topology.

Topology is the arrangement that constrains how point, line, and polygon features share geometry.

In geometry, topology deals with the properties of a figure that remain unchanged even when the figure is bent, stretched, or otherwise distorted. Vector data can vary in scale, accuracy, and quality. We'll come back to this in Topic 2.

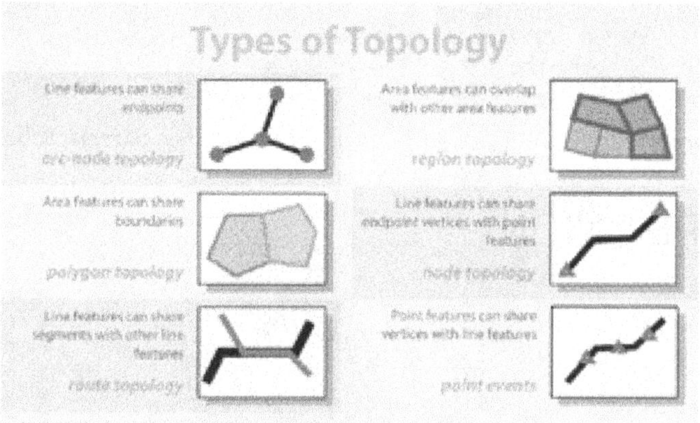

Illustration of types of topology,

Source: http://www.esri.com/news/arcnews/summer02articles/arcgis-brings-topology.html

Vector Data Examples and Applications

Vector data are commonly used for themes that are made of explicit objects, such as parcel ownership data, political boundaries, and streets. Other examples include the following:

Hydrographic data (e.g. rivers, streams)

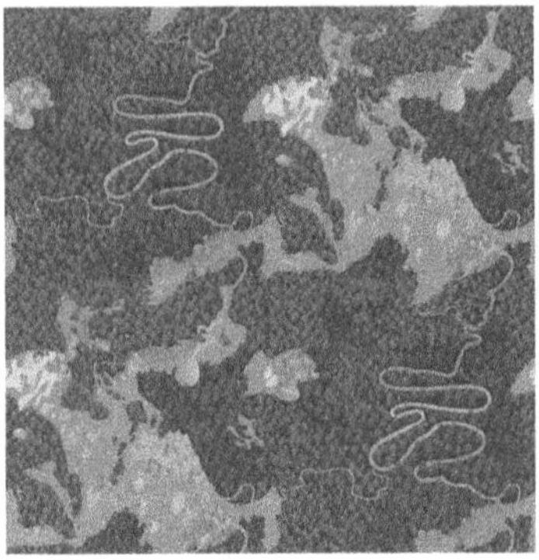

Wetlands

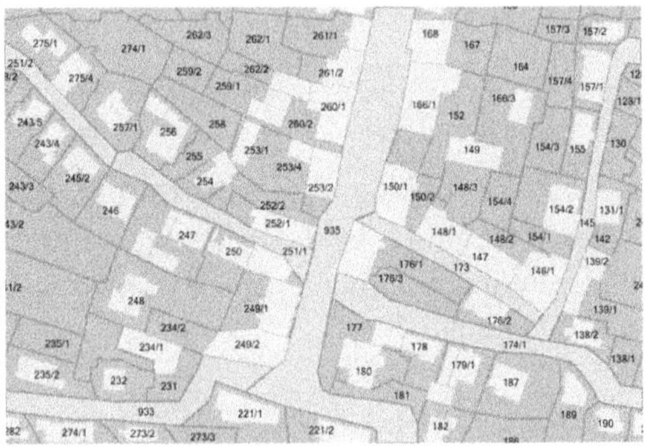

Boundaries, parcels, & buildings

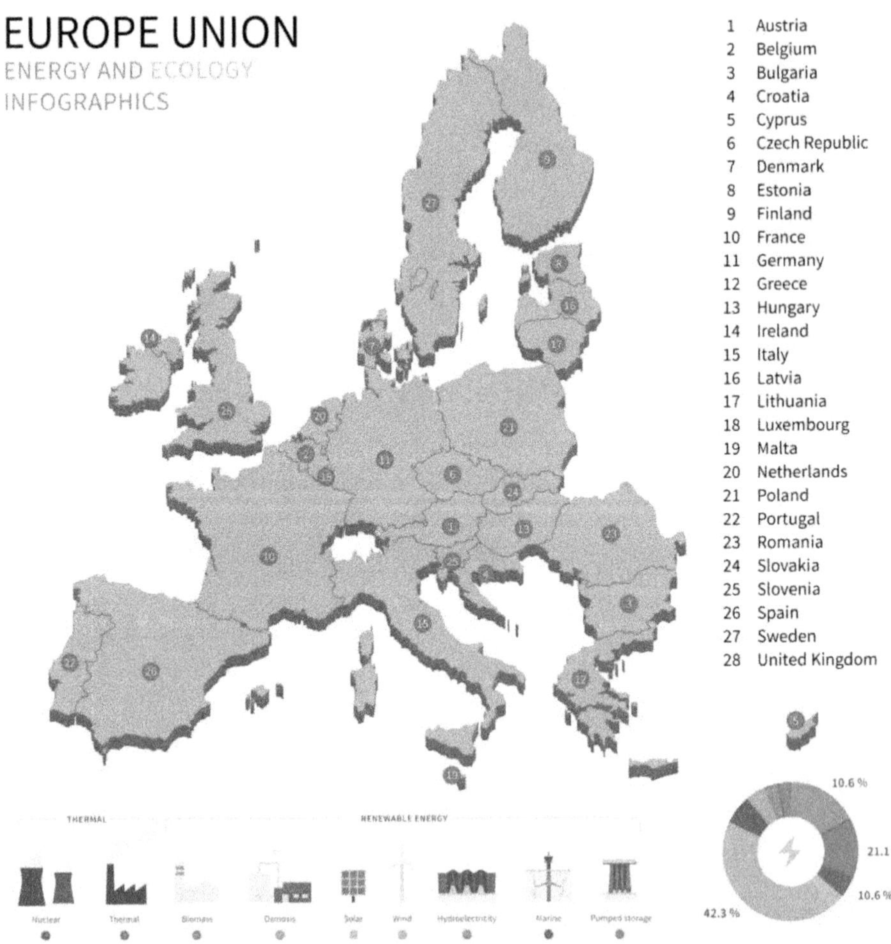

Energy facilities

Geological map of France, vintage engraved illustration. Earth before man 1886.

Geologic & soils boundaries *Images © Shutterstock, Inc.*

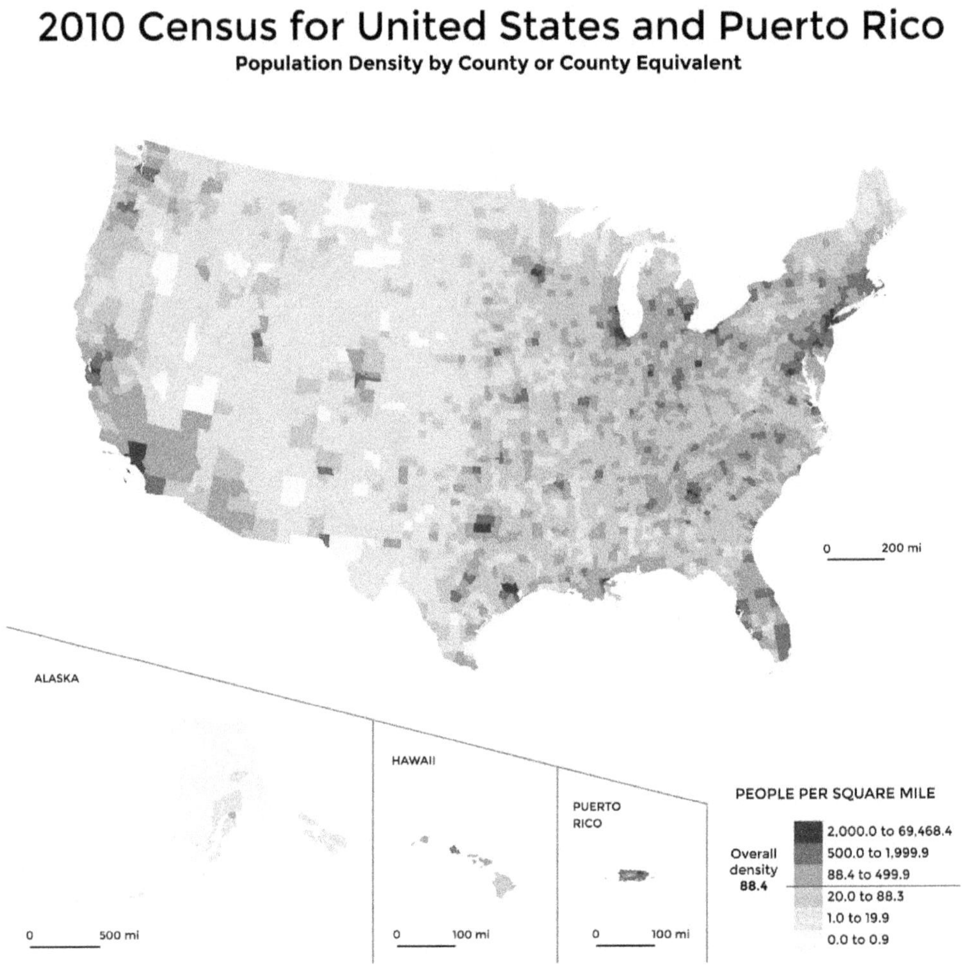

Census 2010 map – population density USA and Puerto Rico

Image © Shutterstock, Inc.

TINs

Triangulated Irregular Networks (TINs) connect points to form triangles that represent facets to efficiently represent complex surfaces.

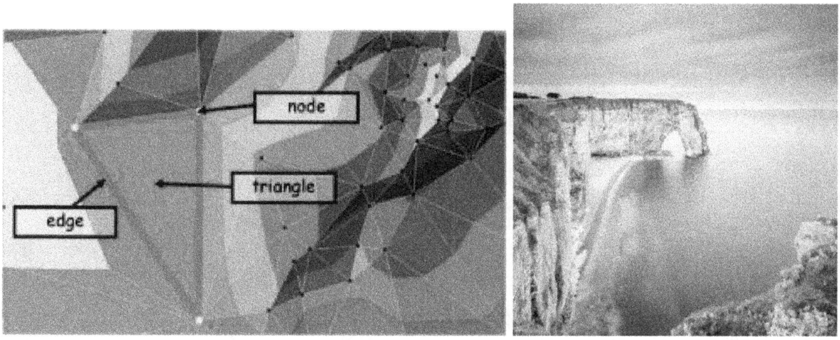

Illustration of TIN data representing elevation.

Source: https://www.pinterest.com/pin/493073859183245047/

Etretat, la Manneporte natural rock arch wonder, cliff and beach. Long exposure photography. Normandy, France. Image © Shutterstock, Inc.

Each data model represents the real world in a different way and is suited to representing specific types of spatial phenomena.

Although TINs are used less often than raster data models, they can more effectively and efficiently describe a surface that has variable change. Imagine a plateau (relatively flat), with a cliff-like drop-off.

Topic 1 Knowledge Check

2. DIGGING INTO RASTER AND VECTOR DATA

Raster and vector data models are more commonly used in natural resource applications than TINs. Yet each data model has its own advantages and disadvantages. The choice of raster or vector structure depends on the following:

- ☆ The nature of the earth surface or features being represented
- ☆ The spatial questions to be asked
- ☆ The kind of data available
- ☆ The software tools to be used

Either data model could be converted to, or overlaid with the other.

The following pages dig into data quality considerations of rasters and vectors, then compare the advantages and disadvantages of each data type, their applications, and considerations for moving between data types.

Data Structure

How the spatial data are structured to represent features on earth influences

- ☆ The level of precision of that spatial data
- ☆ What technology will be used for viewing and analysis
- ☆ How spatial overlays and modeling will be conducted
- ☆ If coordinate transformation or reprojection will be needed

Raster data have a simple data structure that results in large data volume and requires high storage capacity. Topology (or the spatial relationships between objects) cannot be represented in raster data.

Vector data have a compact but complex data structure that enables explicit definition of topology and requires less storage capacity.

Precision

In raster data, object shapes cannot be precisely represented when pixel size is large (resolution is low) because of constraints of the cell shape. Spatial variation can be accommodated through increased spatial resolution.

In vector models, objects can be precisely represented using points, lines, and polygons (areas). However, spatial variation of attributes within a polygon cannot be expressed.

Viewing and Analysis Technology

The simple data structure of cells has allowed the development of inexpensive technology for working with raster data (Bolstad 2016). But the graphical output of raster data products may not be pleasing (e.g., blocky depending on resolution).

On the other hand, due to its complex data structure, technology for viewing and analyzing vector data is more expensive, but graphical output of vector data may be more visually pleasing (smoother edges).

Spatial Overlay and Mathematical Modeling

These analyses are more difficult using vector data, because objects on different layers have different shapes.

On the other hand, modeling and overlay using raster data are easier, because pixels of different layers can be overlaid and added, subtracted, multiplied, and so on.

Coordinate Transformation

In raster data, coordinate transformation (or map projection) often results in loss of information due to resampling of pixels, and projection transformations are more difficult. In vector, coordinate and projection transformations are easier, since every object is defined by points.

Vector to raster conversion. Illustration by Ashley Kissick, 2018.

We often need to convert vector data to raster to run overlay or modeling calculations. Likewise, many geoprocessing operations work best with vector data. Converting from vector to raster can result in data loss due to the following:

- ☆ Cell size
- ☆ The choice of pixel size can result in the loss of spatial data, as large cells can mask spatial variation.
- ☆ Loss of attributes
- ☆ When converting from vector to raster data, only one attribute of the polygons can be used to assign values to the new grid cells. Therefore, other attributes will be lost, or will have to be rejoined.
- ☆ Mixed cell problem
- ☆ Occurs when edge pixels may have a mix of class properties. In vector to raster conversion, the grid cells may span two or more polygons, and the resulting cells can only be assigned to one class. This reduces the spatial accuracy of the resulting data.

Converting from raster to vector can be even uglier, and does not ensure that vector output is more accurate. Neighboring pixels with certain attribute values may get translated into new lines or polygons. After the conversion, many spatial problems are likely to arise requiring intensive editing.

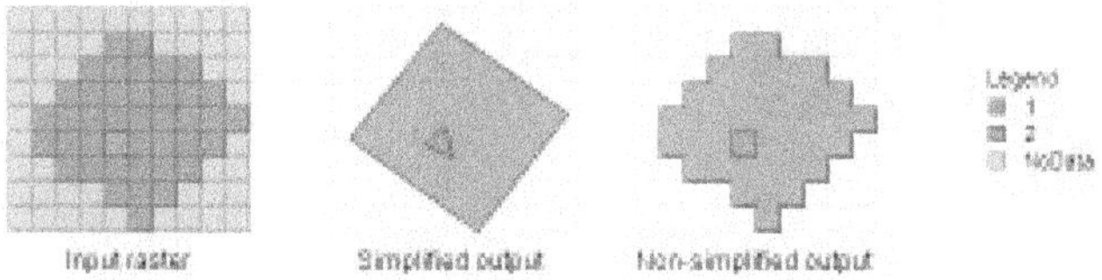

How an input raster is vectorized when converted to a polygon feature output.

http://pro.arcgis.com/en/pro-app/tool-reference/conversion/raster-to-polygon.htm

Vector and Raster in ArcGIS and QGIS

We will work with both vector and raster data in ArcGIS. Many basic geoprocessing tools are designed to work with vector data, whereas raster data processing happens mostly through the spatial analyst extension to:

- ☆ View and overlay raster images
- ☆ Convert between raster and vector
- ☆ Basic spatial analysis with raster data (arithmetic and neighborhood functions)

Vector data in ArcGIS is referred to as Feature Class. We will cover this more in the next lesson.

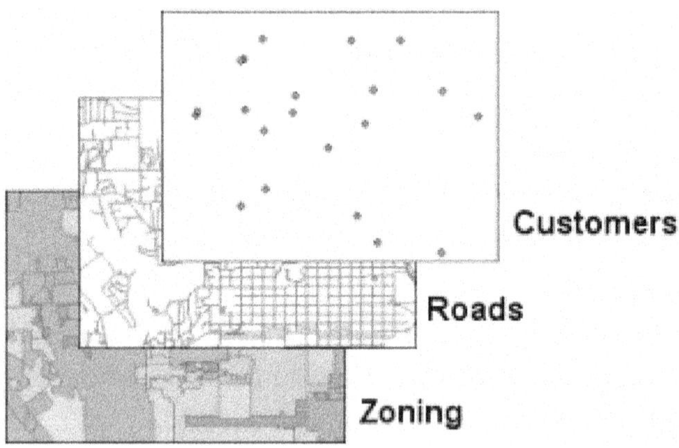

All features in a feature class have the same geometry type, the same attributes, and are located within a common geographic extent.

As you know, raster data in ArcGIS typically use the Esri GRID format.

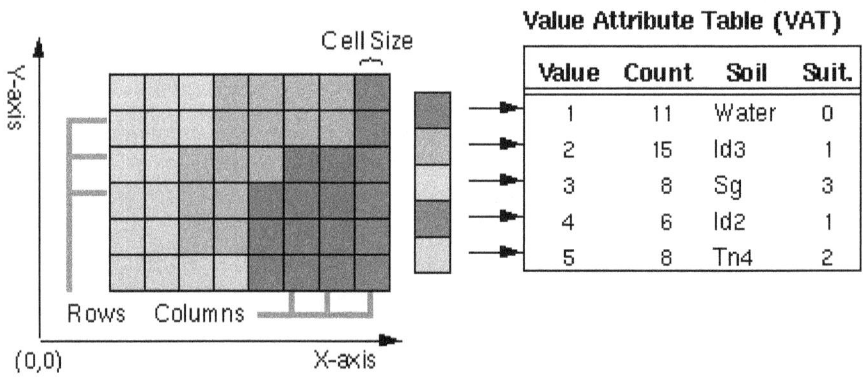

Graphic of raster cells and values.

Since QGIS is open source and built by the community of users, it supports the use of many different raster file formats, including Esri GRID, GeoTIFF, and ERDAS IMAGINE files. The most used geoprocessing tools for raster data are included in the base installation of QGIS Desktop. QGIS also supports a variety of vector data, including Esri shapefiles (https://docs.qgis.org/2.8/en/docs/user_manual/working_with_raster/supported_data.html).

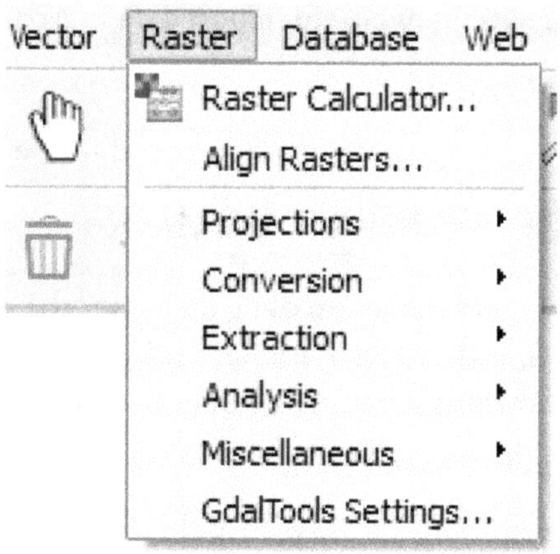

Screenshot of primary raster toolbar in QGIS.

An important difference between ArcGIS and QGIS, is that in QGIS, you must specify if you are importing vector or raster data, whereas ArcGIS does not need prior specification.

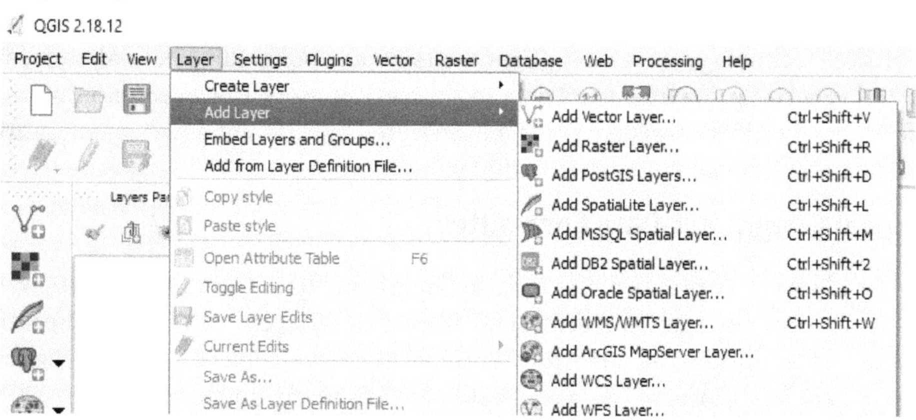

Screenshot of how to import data in QGIS.

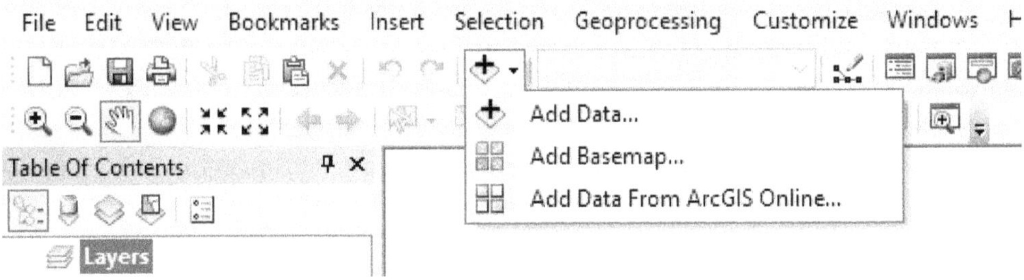

Screenshot of how to import data in ArcGIS

Topic 2 Knowledge Check

Please answer the following questions to proceed to the next topic.

3. SPATIAL DATA IN THE PUBLIC DOMAIN

This topic introduces public domain data, discusses the emergence of the spatial data infrastructure (SDI), introduces national and international portals for spatial data, and covers considerations for utilizing data from these sources.

What is Public Domain Spatial Data?

More and more we can and do rely on publicly available spatial data for GIS analyses. We call this public domain spatial data. In their book, Kerski and Clark (2012, page 10) say you can

"...think of public domain spatial data as publicly accessible information about a spatial theme or phenomenon, the use of which does not infringe the legal rights of an individual or organization."

As GIS technology grew throughout the 1980s as a powerful tool, local, state, and federal agencies provided spatial data to a variety of users. However, duplication of efforts and a lack of consistency in data generated by different government entities made data sharing and integration difficult.

Federal Geographic Data Committee

To address this problem, the Federal Geographic Data Committee (FGDC, www.fgdc.gov), composed of representatives from federal agencies and the Executive Office, was established in 1990 to coordinate the development, use, sharing, and dissemination of geospatial data on a national basis in the United States.

The Federal Geographic Data Committee (FGDC) is an organized structure of federal geospatial professionals and constituents that provide executive, managerial, and advisory direction and oversight for geospatial decisions and initiatives across the federal government.

(www.fgdc.gov, accessed January 23, 2018)

US National Spatial Data Infrastructure

In concert with FGDC, the US **National Spatial Data Infrastructure (NSDI)** was organized to coordinate data standards to reuse and share existing spatial data, and is managed by FGDC. Today, ... *The NSDI leverages investments in people, technology, data, and procedures to create and provide the geospatial knowledge required to understand, protect, and promote our national and global interests.*

(www.fgdc.gov/nsdi/nsdi.html)

The US National Spatial Data Infrastructure NSDI is defined as "the technology, policies, standards, and human resources necessary to acquire, process, store, distribute, and improve utilization of geospatial data."

NSDI Goals

- ☆ **Goal 1** – Develop Capabilities for National Shared Services
- ☆ **Goal 2** – Ensure Accountability and Effective Development and Management of Federal Geospatial Resources
- ☆ **Goal 3** – Convene Leadership of the National Geospatial Community (www.fgdc.gov/nsdi/nsdi.html, accessed January 23, 2018)

Most importantly, these two institutions, FGDC and NSDI, provide consistency in the United States for geospatial data standards and distribution. Not all areas of the world have this level of federal consistency, though global spatial data institutions are growing.

Metadata

Recall—Metadata is information about data. Geospatial metadata describes . . .

- ☆ How, when, where, and by whom the data were collected
- ☆ Availability and distribution of information, projection, scale, resolution, and accuracy
- ☆ Data reliability with regard to some standard

The Content Standard for Digital Geospatial Metadata is the metadata standard developed by the FGDC factsheet [https://www.fgdc.gov/metadata, factsheet].

Metadata functions to . . .

- ☆ Preserve a history of the data
- ☆ Enable users to assess the suitability of data for a project
- ☆ Ensure accountability for data content
- ☆ Document data and project development and processing

Geospatial Platform

Neither the FGDC nor NSDI were set up to distribute geospatial data resources, so a national geospatial data clearinghouse was organized as a virtual repository of geospatial metadata from various government suppliers such as United States Geological Survey (USGS). Today, FGDC provides a portal to these resources:

Geospatial Platform is an FGDC initiative that provides shared and trusted geospatial data, services, and applications. Search our massive catalog of geospatial data and tools provided by a multitude of federal agencies. Whether you are a geographic professional, student, teacher, or citizen, you can find data that will help you with your project, assignment, presentation, or concern.

(www.fgdc.gov/dataandservices, accessed 23 Jan 2018)

Regional versus Thematic Data Portals

Data may be organized geographically, such as portals that contain data pertinent to one state or nation. US national data portals include the following:

- ☆ Geoplatform.gov
- ☆ Data.gov
- ☆ The USGS nationalmap.gov
- ☆ The USDA NRCS data gateway

Alternatively, data may be organized around certain themes, such as the following:

- ☆ The Geo Network of the Food and Agriculture Organization
- ☆ Data Basin by the Conservation Biology Institute (we'll look at this source more soon).
- ☆ And there are more grassroots open source geospatial data portals, such as:
- ☆ Data ONE

International Spatial Data Infrastructure

GSDI
Global Spatial Data
Infrastructure Association

Similarly, a global spatial data infrastructure (GSDI) initiative is also underway to facilitate the creation, maintenance, and sharing of spatial data around the world. This is especially important for projects seeking to address environmental issues that span national and regional boundaries, such as the tsunami that affected many countries in Southeast Asia.

http://gsdiassociation.org/

Image © Shutterstock, Inc.

However, sharing global data across boundaries has additional challenges and inconsistencies in the following:

- ☆ Gaps in spatial data and documentation
- ☆ Incompatible spatial datasets
- ☆ Incompatible GIS
- ☆ Limitations to sharing data

The GSDI Association, a consortium of organizations, agencies, companies, and individuals, promotes international cooperation in support of local, national, and international spatial data infrastructure to better address global, social, economic, and environmental issues.

Our purpose is to encourage international cooperation that stimulates the implementation and development of national, regional, and local spatial data infrastructures.

- ☆ SSDI (gsdiassociation.org, accessed January 23, 2018).

Several standards have been developed for global geospatial data, including those by the International Organization for Standardization, the Open Geospatial Consortium, the World Wide Web Consortium, and others.

A few key international data portals include . . .

- ☆ USGS Planetary GIS Web Server
- ☆ United Nations FAO GeoNetwork
- ☆ UNEP Geo Data Portal

Note that international portals may vary in the ability to view, download, or use spatial data.

We will visit some of these as we go through this book series.

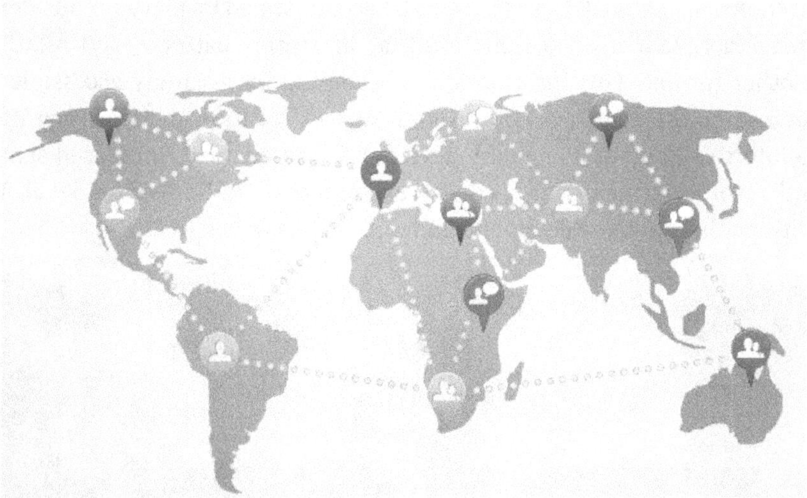

Image © Shutterstock, Inc.

Data Ethics and Politics

Accessing and utilizing spatial data across international boundaries carries special ethical and political considerations.

Spatial data depicting the location of and access to specific natural resources and land use may be contested by neighboring governments.

Roma, TX Winding Rio Grande River separating U.S. and Mexico. The right side is Texas, and the left side is Mexico. Photo by Alan Schmierer, via Wikimedia Commons

Differential access to spatial data also means that some individuals or groups may be at a disadvantage in disputes concerning natural resources, land use or ownership rights, and in access to goods and services.

The choice of spatial data should also be accompanied by privacy considerations. Maps are a rich source of information that illustrates patterns and relationships like no other format. This information is becoming increasingly accessible via the Internet and social media, as traditional sources location data privacy of public data go into the cloud and as many devices are geo-enabled. Increased spatial and temporal resolution means data can be examined at the individual level. We will work with publicly accessible mobile and online data in Lesson 2.

AUCKLAND—DEC 02 2015: Google Street View camera operator at work. It's a technology featured in Google Maps and Google Earth that provides panoramic views from positions along streets in the world. Shutterstock

Meanwhile, privacy laws do not clearly dictate which personal and government data belongs in the public domain, and individual cases are setting precedent on both sides of privacy arguments.

Check out this Spatial Reserves blog on location data privacy by J. Kerski.

- ☆ Topic 3 Knowledge Check
- ☆ Review of Coordinate Systems
- ☆ What is a coordinate System?

A coordinate system is a system that uses a common framework to represent locations of geographic features, observations, and imagery. In other words, a coordinate system provides a method for understanding real-world locations.

There are two main types of coordinate systems: Geographic and Projected

Geographic Coordinate System

A geographic coordinate system uses spherical coordinates (eg. decimal degrees) and measures from the center of a 3D sphere, ie. the center of the earth. Because the surface is spherical, the lengths, angles and areas are not constant, and therefore distances between latitude and longitude lines will change as we move from equator to poles.

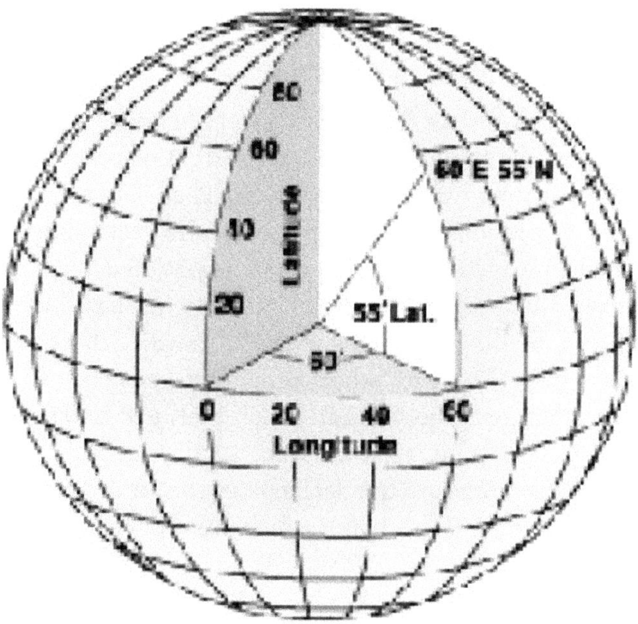

Projected Coordinate System

A projected coordinate system uses planar coordinates (eg. feet, meters, etc) to project the earths spherical surface on to a 2D Cartesian coordinate surface. Projected coordinate systems are always based on Geographic coordinate systems, and the lengths, angles and areas are always constant. In order to make these measurements constant and accurate, projected coordinate systems include a map projection which translates spherical coordinates to planar coordinates using particular parameters that customize the map for a particular location.

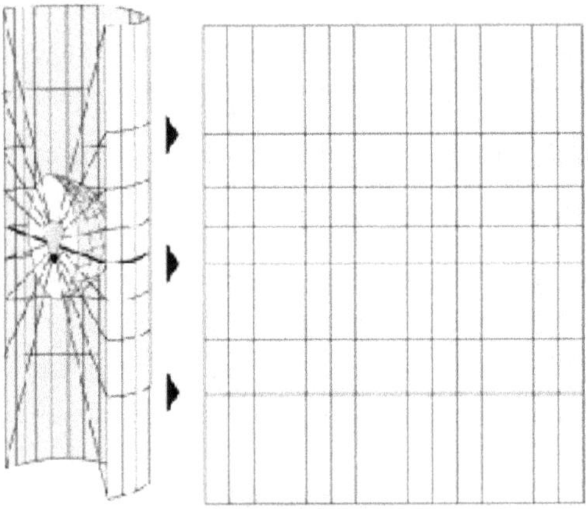

How Does this Translate to ArcMap?

So, how does this translate to what you see in ArcMap? Lets imagine we have a dataset with 100 data-points which represent the locations of wolf-livestock conflicts in Idaho (*i.e.* where wolves have killed livestock). Each data point has a latitude and a longitude value recorded in decimal degrees. Those decimal degrees relate to the geographic coordinate system of those points (eg. WGS-84). So, if we bring those points into ArcMap, the program would know where those points are located on the sphere of Earth. But, in order for you to be able to visualize those points as you would on a flat map (vs. a globe), and with other spatial data, you need to define a projection. Since all the points are in Idaho, you can look for a North American projection, and you may even want something more accurate, such as an Idaho specific projection. The program will then translate the decimal degrees into planar units so that you can accurately examine values such as the distances between points.

Wolves hunting a Bison

To learn more about this, look at ESRI's online course Understanding Map Projections and Coordinate Systems

Media Attributions

- GIS Maps
- GIS
- Badger
- Raster
- Raster Thematic
- Raster Continuous
- Vector data model
- Types of Topology
- Census Map
- TIN
- Beach and Cliffs
- Vector example
- Raster to Vector
- Features
- Fisherman
- World map
- Roma, Texas
- Recording

CHAPTER-2

FEATURE DATA: GETTING FIELD AND CITIZEN OBSERVATIONS INTO DESKTOP AND WEB MAPS

Because some problems are local in nature, we sometimes need to gather and map our own data or observations from others. Here we focus on the kind of data you might gather in the field and how to bring that into a geographic information system (GIS) workspace. These data may come from walking a trail with a global positioning system (GPS) unit, placing a radio collar on a coyote to record its locations, or having citizen scientists enter locational information.

Photo from Madison Urban Canid study, with permission from Dr. David Drake and Marcus Mueller, (photo by Jeff Miller, UW-Madison)

We will also learn how to access real-time data online, and on how to map that data with web mapping tools. Finally, you'll get a taste for sharing spatial data with live web maps through ArcGIS Online.

In this lesson, you:

- ☆ Examine feature data and considerations for collecting field observations
- ☆ Learn how to import field data to feature data in GIS
- ☆ Explore cloud-based mapping and learn how to produce and use online web maps
- ☆ Look at case studies of citizen science GIS and cloud-based maps

Lesson 2 Topics

This lesson covers three topics and takes about 50 minutes to complete. We recommend working through each topic in the order listed below.

- ☆ Collecting feature data in the field
- ☆ Importing field data to your GIS
- ☆ Citizen data and mobile mapping

1. COLLECTING FEATURE DATA IN THE FIELD

Where does environmental data come from? Simply, we can collect observations of the environment from:

- ☆ **On the ground**—we'll call these Field Observations
- ☆ **Above ground (or from some distance)**—referred to as Remote Sensing (more on this later)

Someone or some device on the ground or at sea, recording information about specific places, captures field or place-based observations.

In this lesson, we focus on turning field observations of the earth into spatial data for a GIS.

Former graduate student Marcus Mueller carries a coyote to the research site, (photo by Jeff Miller, UW-Madison)

So, How Are Field Observations Spatial Data?

Imagine the kinds of landscape or environmental data you might want to collect:

- ☆ Stream gauge readings
- ☆ Nocturnal lemur locations
- ☆ Bicycle sharing stations
- ☆ Ice Age Trail additions
- ☆ Urban community gardens
- ☆ Park boundaries

Author collecting data in field with mobile device. Photo from author's collection.	**Bicycle sharing service or rental technology concept**

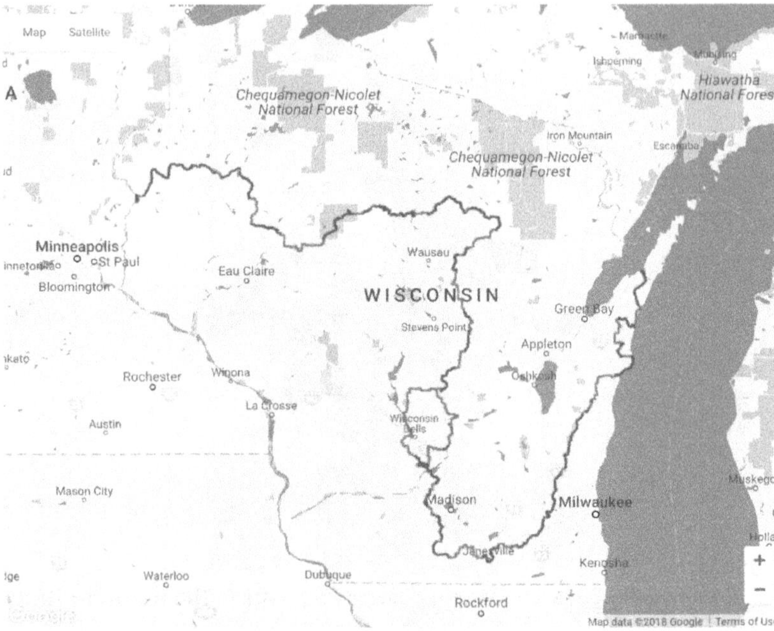

Route of Ice Age National Scenic Trail through Wisconsin, from Ice Age Trail Alliance online map, https://www.iceagetrail.org/trail-maps-guidebooks/

Recording the boundaries of defined regions, parks, and protected areas are represented by polygons.

Photo from author's library

These represent different kinds of landscape **FEATURES.**

So what kind of data models are these features? Let's see, we have . . .

- ☆ *points* of stations
- ☆ *lines* of trail routes
- ☆ *polygons* of park boundaries

Vector data! Feature data in GIS typically refer to vector data in point, line, or polygon format.

What is Feature Data?

Feature **classes** are collections of similar features, each having the same spatial representation, such as points, lines, or polygons, and a common set of attribute fields. For example, in a feature class representing streams each record would be a polyline, or multiple connected line segments, representing a single stream feature, and each would have the same fields of say, name, stream order, and class.

The four most commonly used feature classes are points, lines, polygons, and annotation (or labels).

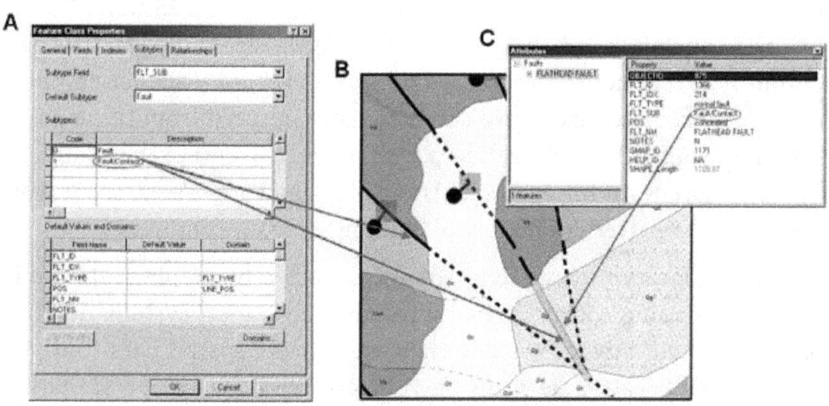

Feature classes, from ArcGIS resource center.

A feature **dataset** is a collection of related feature classes that share a common coordinate and projection system. Feature datasets are used to spatially or thematically integrate related feature classes for building topology or networks. In this case, the stream feature class might be organized with a polygon feature class of lakes and ponds.

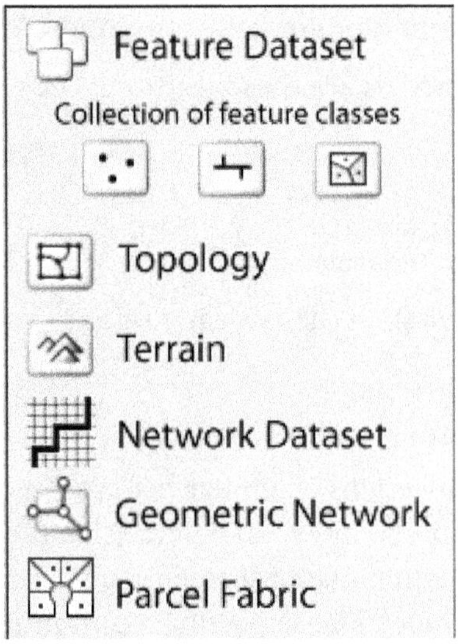

Feature dataset from ArcGIS Resource Center

Collecting Feature Data

We might think of collecting field data with expensive GPS units that we take back to camp to download onto a computer. There are also a wide variety of electronic means, from smartphones to probes and drones, to record place-based phenomena in accessible and remote places. We can map data captured from these devices in a GIS. Examining your gathered field data with a map can reveal the spatial patterns that may be inherent in, for example, tree height and tree species, pH along your local stream, or the pattern of historical buildings in your community.

Today, many location-based data are also collected by tapping into the location signals of people using social media, apps, and navigation systems in their daily lives, usually without any knowledge they are sharing spatial data! Did you know when you turn on Location Services on your phone or for an app you are sharing your location to the cloud? And that crowd-sourced spatial data are real time—it uploads to the cloud or servers automatically and can be immediately available for viewing and analysis. We will look at some ways that location-based data are tapped for geospatial analyses later in this lesson.

There are also approaches for intentional citizen-collected field data, where the citizens are informed, willing, and engaged with the spatial data being collected (e.g., Christmas bird count), as opposed to harvested crowd-sourced data. We will come back to some approaches for citizen-collected field data with mobile devices shortly. First, let us work with some data collected from probes or receivers that you wish to import into GIS.

Citizens collecting field observations with mobile app in Duluth-Superior area, USA. Photo from author's library.

Methods of Data Gathering, Mapping, and Analysis

Before collecting spatial data in the field, evaluate the project goals, the time and equipment available, terrain, signal reception, and other factors that might influence your spatial accuracy and the usefulness of your data. Planning is essential for efficient field collection of good spatial data to address your question or goal.

Some key considerations and steps to consider before location-based fieldwork are the following:

- ☆ Know what type of sensors or receivers will be used for data collection;
- ☆ Determine the sampling design, including the route and frequency of recordings;

- ☆ Identify the attribute data to be collected.

For example, if you are surveying birds by song along a transect, what devices will you use to record location and audio? What is your transect route? How frequently will you stop to listen and identify, and what characteristics of that observation will you record (forest type, canopy cover, bird species, human disturbance, etc.)—these are the attributes for each record in your spatial database.

Keep in mind your field observations might come from: a pencil and clipboard at known permanent plots, GPS receivers, telemetry, drones, soil probes, energy meters, lake level sensors, smartphones, social media feeds, and many more means and devices.

Field equipment for St. Louis River Estuary, Duluth-Superior area, USA. Photo from author's library.

Reflection

How have you gathered data in the field in the past? Maybe you:

- ☆ recorded plant species at a site
- ☆ took pictures with a drone
- ☆ took stream temperature measurements
- ☆ checked the water level at beaches along Lake Michigan
- ☆ helped track the mountain lions in Los Angeles
- ☆ captured community response to streambank flooding.

Recording coastal plant information along Lake Superior. Photo from author's library.

Each of these kinds of field observations can be spatially located. Think about the kind of attribute information that might be collected with these spatial field data. How would you do it differently if you had access to the best equipment today?

2. IMPORTING FEATURE DATA INTO YOUR GIS

Most GIS (*e.g.*, QGIS, ArcGIS desktop, Pro, online) tools, and some other web maps (*e.g.*, GoogleEarth) can be used to map the data that you have gathered. A mapping toolset requires that the data being mapped have a geolocation attached to it—a city/state, zip code, street address, UTM or a latitude–longitude coordinate pair.

Sometimes spatial data require transformation before they can be utilized within spatial analysis. There are many free packages available online that can be downloaded to convert spatial datasets to the appropriate file type. Many handheld GPS files collect point data as a .gpx file, which must be converted to a different point file format, such as a text or comma delimited (csv) file with X,Y coordinates for use within a GIS.

Backpacker with GPS navigator looking for coordinates.

Adding X,Y Coordinate Data as a Layer

X,Y coordinates describe points on the earth's surface such as the location of fire ignites in the desert grasslands or the points where water samples were collected in an estuary. Frequently we collect X,Y coordinate data with an elevation [Z]-value.

You can add field observations that contain geographic locations in the form of X,Y coordinates to your map. If the table also contains Z-coordinates, such as elevation, depth, or temperature for example, you can add these data as three-dimensional attributes into your map.

Initially when you add location-based data to your map as a table it becomes an X,Y event layer and behaves like other point feature layers, but does not have all the functionality of a feature class yet.

Attributes of points_utm

FID	Shape*	X	Y
0	Point	-79.235444	43.207055
1	Point	-79.261247	43.191196
2	Point	-79.205194	43.149254
3	Point	-79.207431	43.147622
4	Point	-79.215648	43.15465
5	Point	-79.250881	43.164771
6	Point	-79.253802	43.170664
7	Point	-79.267453	43.155617
8	Point	-79.2638	43.16129
9	Point	-79.21237	43.139409
10	Point	-79.244187	43.12796
11	Point	-79.196958	43.134143
12	Point	-79.212195	43.132831
13	Point	-79.279129	43.170963

Record: 1 Show: All Selected Records (0 out of 14 Selected.) Options

Screen capture of X,Y event table added in ArcGIS

To add a table of X,Y coordinates to your map, the table must contain two fields: one for the X-coordinate, representing east-west location, and one for the Y-coordinate, reflecting the north-south position. The values in the fields may represent any coordinate system and units such as latitude and longitude or meters. A field for the Z-coordinates that enables 3D geometry is optional and will be in either metric or English units (meters or feet).

The fields must be decimal numerals. If the coordinate values are stored in degrees, minutes, and seconds (e.g., 118° 24' 46") they must be converted and displayed as decimal degrees (= 118.4128°). If working with Z-coordinates, you can also change properties such as the layer's vertical exaggeration or its offset from an elevation surface.

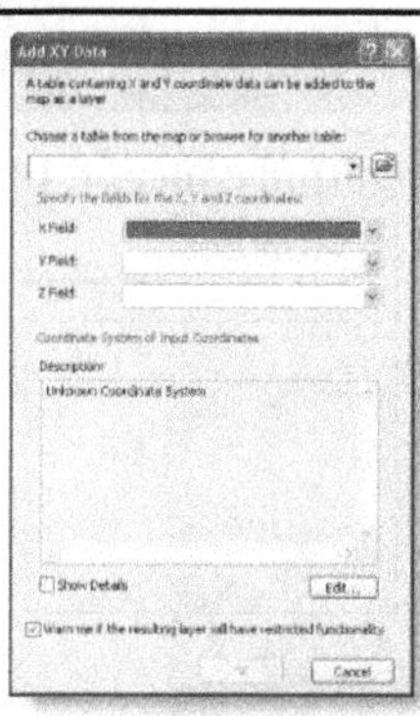	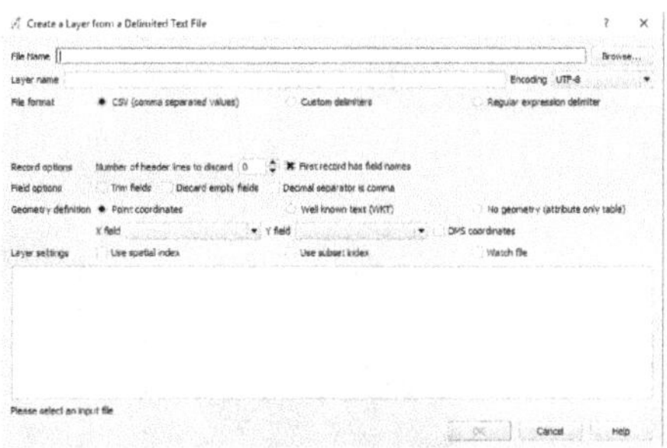
Pop-up window for adding X,Y data in ArcGIS	**Adding x,y data saved in a text file as a point layer in QGIS.**

Know Your Data

When importing feature data from the field, it is especially important to know how it was collected. For a dramatic example of what happened when mapping Lyme disease in Rhode Island, check out the video below, and read the Directions Magazine article that accompanies this lesson.

Know your data! Example from mapping Lyme Disease

3. CITIZEN DATA AND MOBILE MAPPING

We are in an era where just about everything around us is "geo-enabled." From our smartphones to our tablets, from webcams recording traffic or bird counts to whether car park lots are empty or full, from Earth-imaging satellites orbiting above us, to sensors below us tracking storms at sea, all of these sensors and devices are transmitting a locational coordinate signal, enabled by the coupling of GPS, smartphone towers, and Wi-Fi transmitters. Geo-enabling is being extended to thermostats, light switches, and appliances in our very own homes, fostering what is known as "the Internet of things" and "smart cities" (Al-Hader and Rodzi 2009).

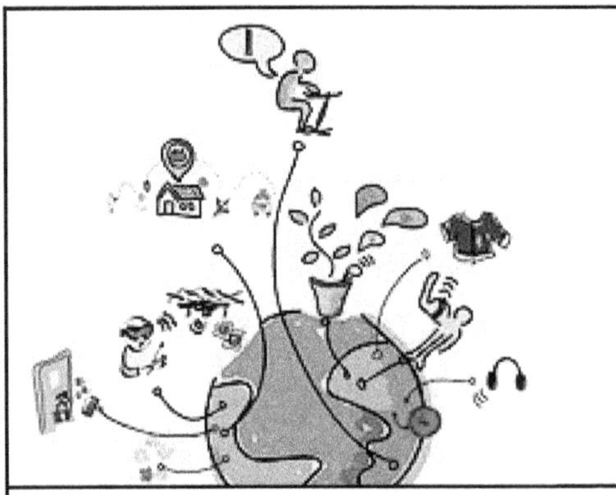

Drawing representing the Internet of Things, Wikipedia

Mobile GPS navigation concept. Image © Gettyimages

Hand Holding Mobile Phone Booking Taxi. Image © Gettyimages

Harvesting citizen data

Sometimes the data transmitted by these devices unknowingly (e.g. car navigation systems support traffic reporting), or intentionally posted (e.g. via Twitter, Instagram) can be harvested by spatially savvy analysts to identify patterns in peoples' lives. For example, colleagues at the Swiss Federal Institute for Forest, Snow, and Landscape Research (WSL) are accessing 1000s of photos and tags on Flicker to learn about cultural perspectives of Swiss landscapes (Dunkel, A 2015). Relatedly, another in England has tapped the platform 'Geographe' to capture users' sense of place (Purves, et al 2011).

Citizen Scientists and Volunteered Geographic Information

On the other hand, often citizens are motivated to voluntarily collect geospatial data as a part of the broader **citizen science** context and is referred to as **volunteered geographic information (VGI)** and **participatory or community mapping** in the world of GIS. These VGI collectors might be avid birders, conservation-oriented hunters, or residents concerned about lakeshore erosion for example.

Let's look at several examples of citizen science initiatives to collect location-based observations. Click the links below to explore a few now:

- ☆ National Audubon Great Backyard Bird Count
- ☆ iNaturalist
- ☆ Open Street Map

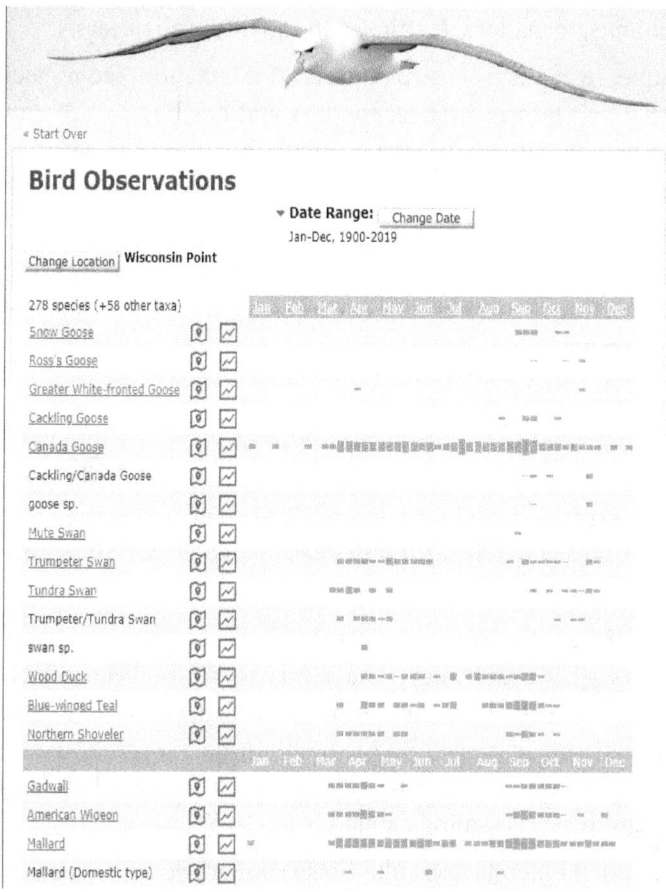

Crowd sourced bird count information website. Screenshot from https://ebird.org

Citizen Mapping Networks Respond!

Citizen-collected spatial data, or VGI, can also provide critical information needed for disaster relief, distribution of humanitarian aid, community development, health, and education. For example, MapAction is a nongovernmental organization (NGO) made up of volunteer GIS professionals that rapidly gather on-the-scene georeferenced information to create maps that facilitate the timely delivery of humanitarian aid in areas affected by natural disasters.

Prince Harry shines a light on the vital work of MapAction volunteers (links to video above)

Likewise, VGI is increasingly used by authoritative sources, such as government agencies and private companies, to create near-real-time maps to inform situation monitoring and emergency response, such as monitoring wildfires, volcanic eruptions, tsunamis, tornadoes, traffic, water quality, and others.

For example, Esri uses crowd-sourced information from social media to create maps that can inform first responders and has hosted VGI-contributed web applications for many natural disasters. Google has also used search terms to map the outbreak and spread of the flu, which informs doctors and hospitals of trends in patient illness.

In China, increased accessibility of social media such as Weibo made a huge difference in reporting of more recent earthquake victims and dangers compared to the Wenchuan earthquake in 2008.

Tracking Social Activities

VGI is also used to create social networks of place for fun and fitness. Similar to FitBits, for example, Map My Tracks uses GPS-enabled mobile devices and a Google map-based app to track all kinds of outdoor fitness and activities. You can challenge and share your routes with friends. Routes are uploaded to a community map shared by all users, similar to Map My Run or Map My Ride.

Likewise, Esri has its own mobile apps. Collector GIS is a map-centric tool, meaning it starts with a web map, and tends to be used more in organizations, whereas Survey123 is called a form-centric tool that allows individuals to write a series of questions to be "surveyed" in the field, stored in a spreadsheet and displayed in a web map after collection. Training videos and tutorials for both of these apps are available through the Esri training catalog.

Many citizen-held mobile apps like these connect your mapped observations to ArcGIS Online, Google Earth/Maps, or other cloud mapping services.

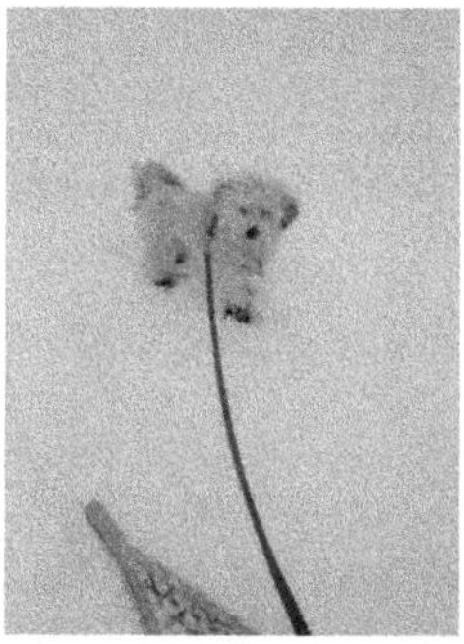

Photo by author of her dog, Chewy

Screen grab from MapMy Tracks

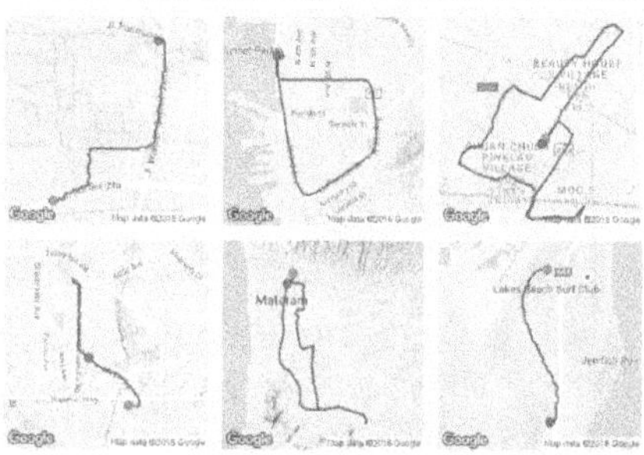

Map data from Google Maps with mapped runs

ArcGIS Collector and Survey123

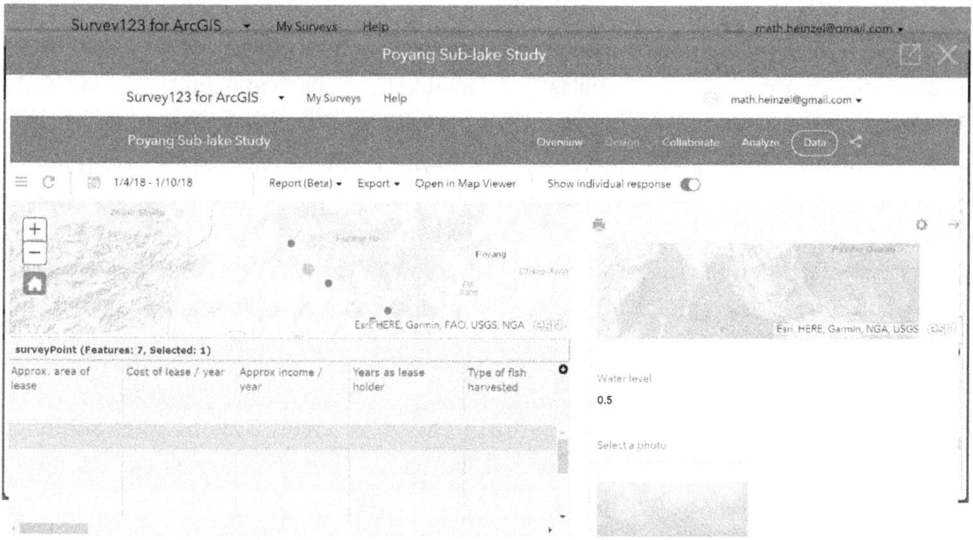

Screens-hots showing observations of fishers in China collected with Survey123, from author's library.

ArcGIS Online provides a robust GIS backbone for viewing and sharing spatial data with the public or password-protected groups as well as cartographic quality mapmaking. Analytical capabilities in ArcGIS online are advancing, adding more functionality regularly.

To learn more about ArcGIS Online, visit this link and click "Learn more about ArcGIS" in the middle of the page.

ArcGIS Online welcome page screenshot

Community Mapping Initiatives

When combined, mobile mapping tools and web-based GIS tools can enable community members to share spatially referenced data with one another and create place-based stories around specific topics. For example, in a Directions Magazine article (2016), Kerski talks about Storytelling as one of five forces catapulting geography onto the world stage. Storymaps are a tool to share your spatial stories with the world. Storymaps grew out of an idea by former National Geographic writer/ photographer, Allen Carroll, called Geostories to beautifully illustrate through maps and photographs the stories of places. Now with Esri, Carroll's team has created a variety of storymap templates that allow people with little to know GIS capability to map and illustrate their own stories.

Similarly, Google Earth has a platform called Voyager. This is an example of their partnership with The Jane Goodall Institute. These initiatives can facilitate citizen science, place-based learning, and community capacity building among other things. We designed a similar customized tool to capture citizens' local experiential knowledge of place. Their individual observations then accumulate through the app to create a community's own spatial narrative (an earlier variation of the Storymap idea). The **Wisconsin Geotools** were piloted in the Green Bay, Wisconsin area, and are under redevelopment for new applications.

To learn more, see Eanes et al. 2018, and the project site here: here

Screenshot by author of spatial narrative geotool.

REFERENCES

Thanks to V.Pfeiffer for contributing content to: Citizen Mapping Networks Respond!

Eanes, F., J.Silbernagel, et al. 2018. Participatory mobile- and web-based tools for eliciting landscape knowledge and perspectives: introducing and evaluating the Wisconsin Geotools Project. J.Coastal Conservation. doi.org/10.1007/s11852-017-0589-2

Kerski, Joseph and Jill Clark. 2012. The GIS Guide to Public Domain Data. Esri Press. 388 pp., http://esripress.esri.com/display/index.cfm?fuseaction=display&websiteID=219&moduleID=0

Kerski, J. 2016. Five forces catapulting geography onto the world stage. Directions Magazine, January, https://www.directionsmag.com/article/1177

Kerski, J. 2015. Why data quality matters — now more than ever. Directions Magazine, August, https://www.directionsmag.com/article/1213

Purves, R., Edwardes, A. and Wood, J. (2011). Describing Place through User Generated Content. First Monday, pp.Volume 16, Number 9-5.

Dunkel, A. (2015). Visualizing the perceived environment using crowdsourced photo geodata. Landscape and Urban Planning 142, pp.173-186. Available at: http://www.elsevier.com/locate/landurbplan.

CHAPTER-3

ASKING SPATIAL QUESTIONS AND MODELING A SPATIAL PROBLEM

In this lesson, you will:

- ☆ Be able to correctly identify the kind of spatial questions to ask, or being asked in a given problem
- ☆ Recognize considerations in planning a geographic information system (GIS) project, such as choosing data, toolsets, output needs, and ethical or error issues
- ☆ Select and use appropriate GIS tools to solve basic environmental spatial questions
- ☆ Identify a series of spatial questions and link them together logically (geoprocess thinking)
- ☆ Learn to build and run a basic geoprocessing model using ModelBuilder

Lesson 3 Topics

This lesson covers three topics and takes approximately 50 minutes to complete. We recommend working through each topic in the order in which they are listed below.

- ☆ Asking Spatial Questions
- ☆ Geoprocess Thinking
- ☆ Using ModelBuilder

1. ASKING SPATIAL QUESTIONS

Despite what you may think, making maps is not the ultimate goal in your GIS education, at least not here. Watch this video by Kerski to see why:

https://youtu.be/qrHoVHq_Ag0

As Kerski said, our goal with GIS is to better understand our world and environment. To do so, we ask spatial questions about the parts of the world we are exploring. Here are the kinds of questions we can ask with GIS:

Location

Where is it? Find the location of all National Parks in South Africa.

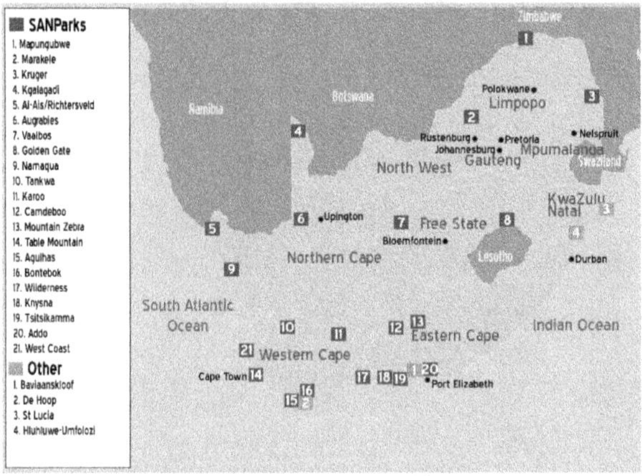

South Africa national park map

Measurement

How far is it? Find the distance between Madison and Kettle Moraine State Park.

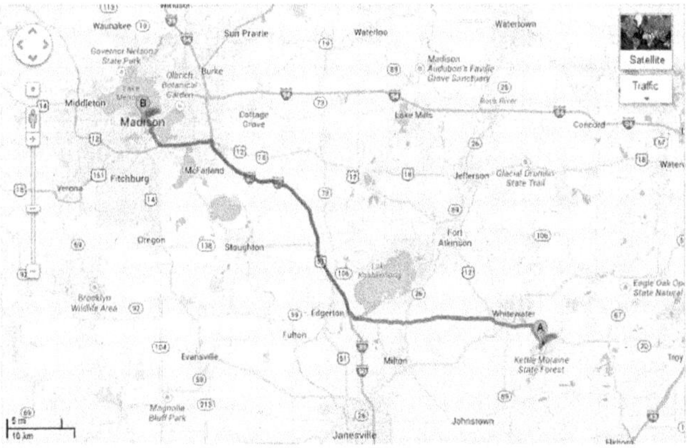

Google maps route by J. Price **48.7 miles!**

Condition

What location fits specific conditions?

Find out which Ontario Parks have cross country skiing trails.

A young woman cross country skiing in Ontario, Canada

Proximity

What is near it? Find out which Wisconsin State Parks are within 20 miles of the Wisconsin River.

Wisconsin River sandwiched between two rocks, Wisconsin Dells, USA

Trends

What has changed since...? Find out where Wisconsin's population has changed since 1990.

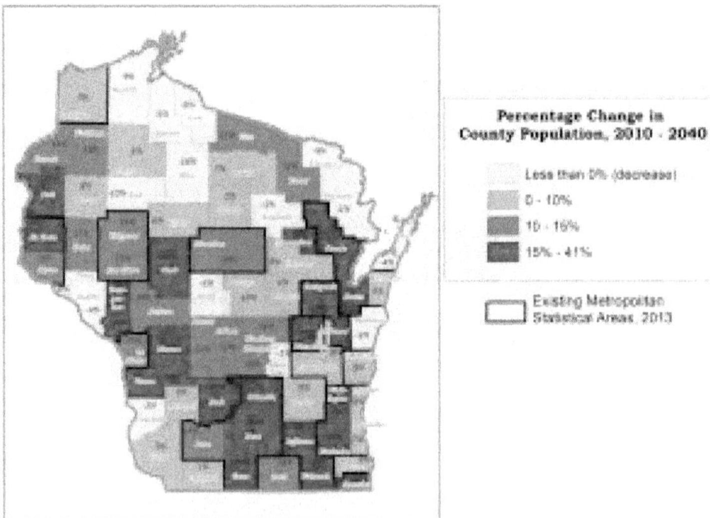

Wisconsin's Future Population Projections for the State, Its Counties, and Municipalities, 2010-2040.

Pattern

What spatial patterns exist? Find out if Wisconsin State Parks are clustered in certain regions such as the Driftless Area, or in areas of steep terrain.

Wyalusing State Park

Routing

Which is the best way? Find the shortest route to the St. Gotthard Pass in the Swiss Alps.

ANDERMATT, SWITZERLAND—June 21, 2015: The railroad bridge Teufelsbruecke—Devil's bridge.The Schollenen Gorge is an important route and the shortest transit to the St. Gotthard Pass

Modeling

What if...? New Zealand wanted to create a new recreational park. Based on land cover, proximity to water, and characteristics most commonly sought by park visitors, where would be best location to create a new state park? What if specific features were prioritized differently—like proximity to an urban population?

Landscape view of recreational park with pathways, lake, and small jetty with blur tree due to wind at Huka Falls, New Zealand

Asking a Spatial Question

Asking a spatial question is the first step in GIS-based project planning. Often spatial questioning is an **iterative process**, where insights into the original question lead to additional, related questions that may be important to making informed decisions.

Carefully framing spatial questions **will lead you to identify the best data** to be gathered, explored, and analyzed. Often we have a great spatial dataset and try to frame questions around it so we can use GIS. Rather, it is more efficient to understand your spatial problem first, and then decide what tools and data you need to best solve it. It is really important to ask yourself, **which data are most relevant to your questions, and to know when you have enough!**

Then when selecting data for your project, you can use the data portals and metadata to consider the following:

- ☆ the original source, medium, format, and purpose of the data
- ☆ the projection, spatial and temporal resolution, and extent of the data
- ☆ the accuracy and reliability of the data
- ☆ the relevance of attributes to spatial question
- ☆ the accessibility and cost of the data

For a detailed list of considerations, see pages 238 and 239 of Kerski and Clark (2012).

Obtaining Spatial Data

Once we've determined our spatial question, we need to identify the spatial data we'll need to answer or analyse our question.

As we covered in Lesson 2, sometimes, especially for more remote areas or unique spatial information, we may need to create and import our own spatial data.

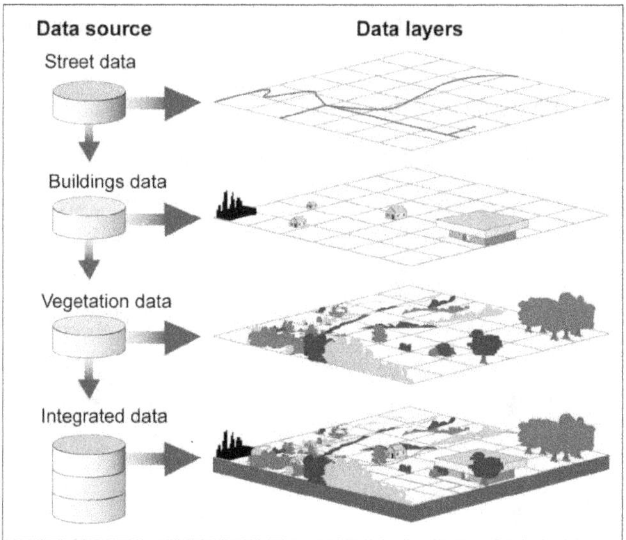

Source: GAO.

Vector Illustration of GIS Spatial Data Layers Concept for Business Analysis, GIS, Icons Design, Liner Style

Very often though, existing data can fulfill the requirements. Acquiring public domain data can be much less time consuming and expensive than capturing new data.

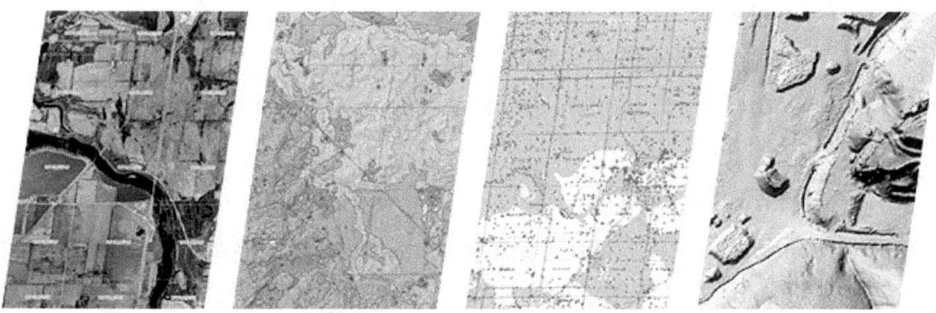

https://clearinghouse.isgs.illinois.edu, accessed January25, 2018

ILLINOIS GEOSPATIAL DATA CLEARINGHOUSE

Public domain data can be obtained from a variety of sources as we learned in Lesson 1, and do not always reside online. Geospatial one-stops and government or university map library collections provide access to a great deal of spatial data. Other offline and informal tools to locate relevant spatial data include the following:

- ☆ consulting the literature to find out which data similar studies or projects used
- ☆ contacting the data provider directly
- ☆ checking with local civic planning offices and community groups
- ☆ and grassroots mapping organizations like "Use-It"

☆ *Logo for USE-IT app https://www.use-it.travel/cities*

Choice of Software

The spatial questions and data inform the **choice of software** to be used. Appropriate software, whether proprietary (e.g., ArcGIS) or open source (e.g., QGIS), will:

- ☆ enable you to work with the data input for the project
- ☆ have the needed display and analytical functionality
- ☆ provide appropriate access (sharing), or not (security)
- ☆ support the output formats necessary to generate required end products
- ☆ fit the project's budget
- ☆ be accompanied by the appropriate level of user support

Both the spatial question and choice of software will help determine who will carry out data acquisition, analysis, and delivery of final products. Careful planning at each of these steps will help balance efforts toward data acquisition with those toward data analysis.

2. GEOPROCESS THINKING

Geoprocessing

Now we will dig into spatial thinking a little deeper. Geoprocessing refers to a framework, tool, or set of functions to query and manipulate spatial data. Geoprocessing allows for spatial data questions or problems to be addressed. Let us see how:

Basically, one or more input spatial datasets goes through a single geoprocessing tool, resulting in a new transformed output layer. Individually these tools perform small but necessary steps, such as "buffer" or "select feature" to move your spatial data from one form to another.

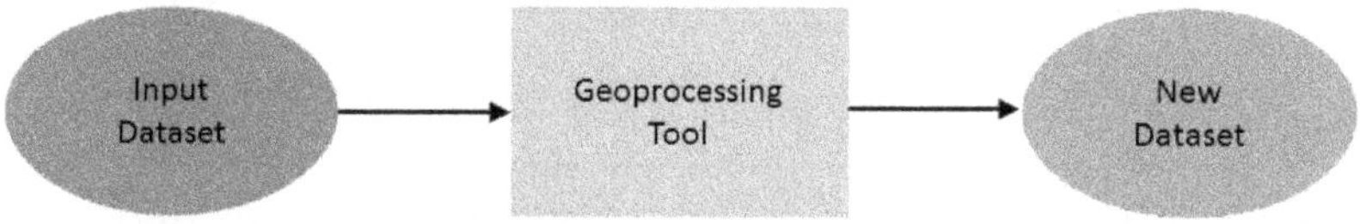

]ArcGIS geoprocessing diagram, from http://resources.esri.com/help/9.3/arcgisengine/arcobjects/esriGeoprocessing/Geoprocessing_overview.htm

We can link a series of geoprocessing tools together and save the process to run it over and over again with different input data or parameters.

Chaining together a series of spatial data and geoprocessing tools creates a geoprocessing model, where the output of one step feeds the input for the next function. Geoprocess models become incredibly useful when working with multiple data layers (e.g., a time sequence of land cover) to analyze complex spatial relationships and reveal new insights. And, they can even be automated to run iterations with batch input or parameters. For example, a geoprocess model could be used to identify areas most prone to landslides over time in a developing area by inputting a time series of development maps and iteratively changing the slope criteria to see how the output areas change.

Geoprocessing Examples

Lets take a look at a few examples of geoprocessing applications.

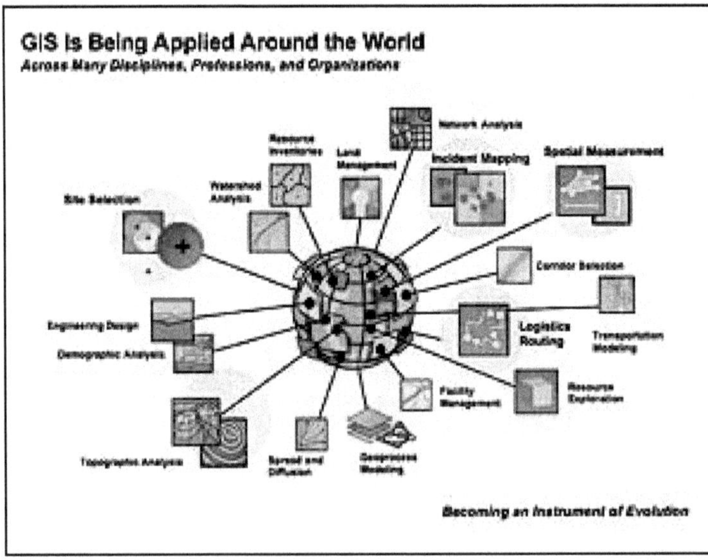

GIS applied around the World. https://www.esri.com/news/arcnews/fall07articles/gis-the-geographic-approach.html

Locating a Pipeline Corridor or Landfill

Spatial Question: What areas would be in some proximity of a proposed pipeline and could be affected by it?

Use the **buffer tool** to select the area within a chosen distance of the proposed pipeline pathway to identify ecologically and socially vulnerable areas and understand environmental justice implications.

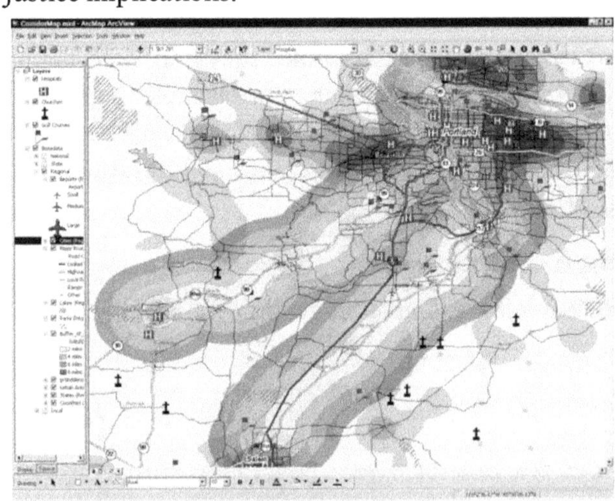

Identifying areas in proximity to a proposed pipeline

Spatial Question: What areas meet certain conditions identified as important for the location of a new landfill?

To identify the suitable locations for a landfill, use the **overlay tool** to identify locations in which slope, distance from water and other landfills, and certain land use types coincide.

- ☆ Each criteria must be carefully selected
- ☆ Decide if each receives equal weight. If not, which gets more? How much more?
- ☆ Think about any uncertainty in these criteria and how that might affect decisions for park placement

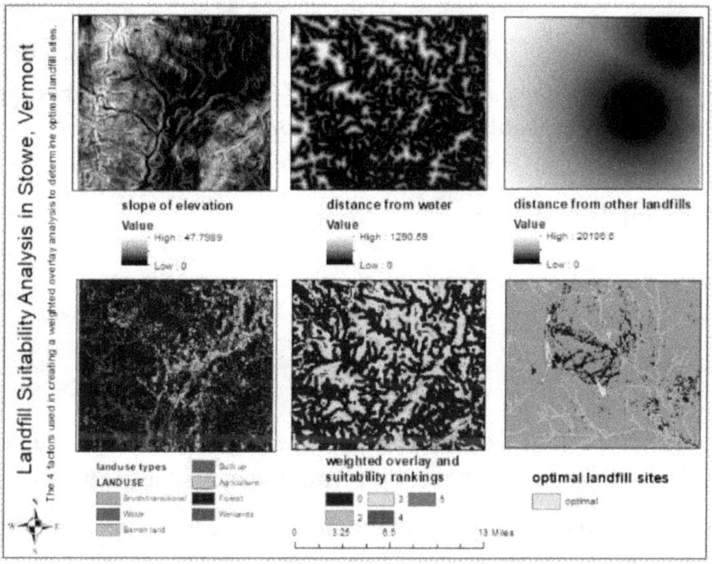

Weighted overlay output for landfill siting. Map by Tyler Gatti, Environmental Conservation GIS student, 2018.

Recommended Fertilizer Application

Spatial Question: A farmer has a limited amount of fertilizer for her hops crop. Where should she apply it?

Determine the spatial pattern of soil nutrient deficiency by mapping soil nutrient data and **selecting by area** where nutrient availability, for example, potassium (K), is lower than the minimum recommended levels for her crop of hops.

*Smart agriculture, precision farming concept. Nea***r-infrared (NIR) images application screen used to create field health maps using the normalize difference vegetation percent index in field rice.**

Geoprocessing Operations

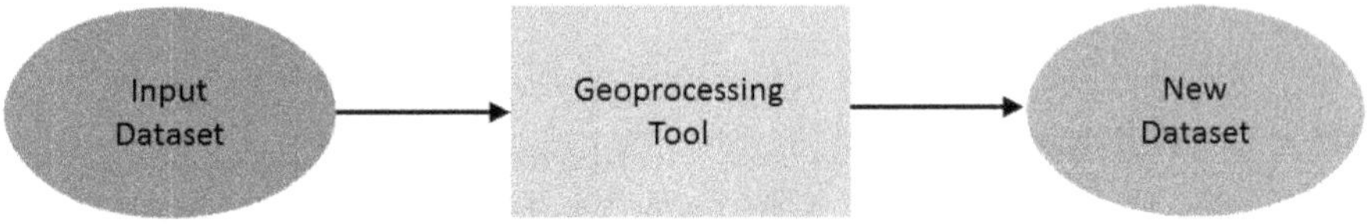

In each of the previous examples, geoprocessing operations were performed in specific sequences to answer the question from the available input data.

Specifically, **geoprocessing tools** take input spatial data, perform a specific operation on those data, and return the result as an output dataset. For instance, you might have two input layers which you "intersect" in geoprocessing to return a single output layer.

Often operations may focus on selecting areas that fit specific criteria, such as selecting for certain attributes, clipping to a boundary, or defining a proximity. You will learn more about specific geoprocessing operations in Topic 3. First, there are some considerations for geoprocessing . . .

Accuracy

When we start combining different spatial data in geoprocessing operations, inaccuracies in the input layers can impact the output. Recall that the accuracy of spatial data is the fidelity with which the data represent real-world phenomena. Accuracy of spatial data can be reduced by:

- ☆ Measurement error
- ☆ Projection distortion
- ☆ Abstraction of real-world objects
- ☆ Generalization
- ☆ Classification
- ☆ Natural variability

Therefore, when combined, the **error of each input dataset propagates** to the output data.

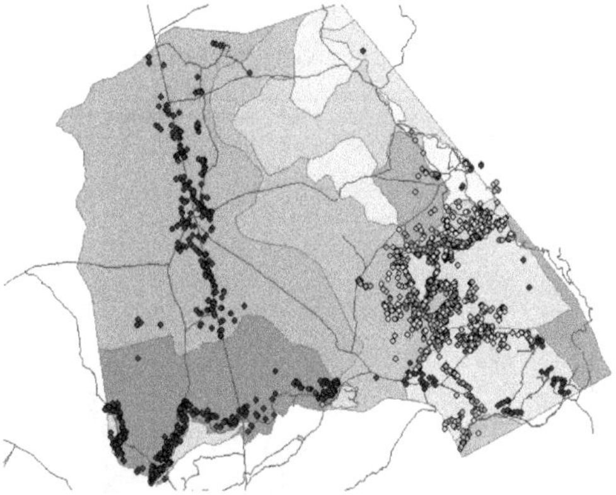

Spatial data on lions and villages in Kenya, shared with author.

Addressing Uncertainty

Due to the inevitable inaccuracy of input data, the output data resulting from geoprocessing operations are inherently uncertain. Therefore, geoprocessing operations ideally should consider OR quantify uncertainty to assess the effect on the resulting conclusions.

If data are not accurate, **errors are propagated** and the uncertainty grows with each geoprocessing step, which affects the accuracy of the results.

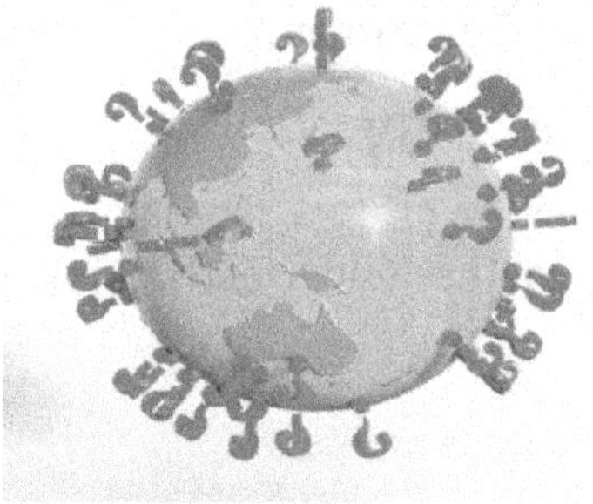

Uncertainty accumulates with each input layer and geoprocessing step.

Sensitivity Analysis

To evaluate uncertainty and explore what happens from your geoprocessing steps, a sensitivity analysis is recommended. Sensitivity analyses simply run multiple iterations of the same geoprocessing steps using different variables to investigate how a process and resulting output respond to changes in input information. For example, changing the slope criteria from 0%–5% to 0%–10% in a site suitability model, or the buffer distance from a hurricane path in a vulnerability model might lead to very different suitable/vulnerable areas in the output.

Sensitivity analyses help us understand the relationships between input and output, estimate how much variability the model produces for each change in the inputs, and identifies which input source contributes most strongly to the output.

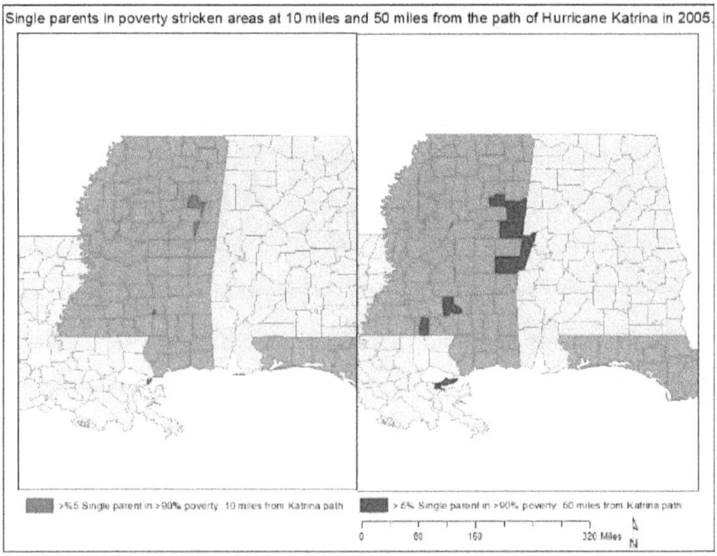

Sensitivity analysis by Matthew Wallrath, Environmental Conservation GIS student, 2018.

The following scenario illustrates how spatial questioning, geoprocess thinking, and sensitivity analysis are combined to inform decision-making.

Gnatcatcher Habitat Suitability

A local land trust wishes to protect habitat for the gnatcatcher, a bird of conservation concern. To do so, they undertake the following activities:

- ☆ Formulate a Spatial Question
- ☆ Summarize Habitat Requirements
- ☆ Obtain Spatial Data

- ☆ Geoprocessing
- ☆ Sensitivity Analysis

And this is what they know about the bird:

Gnatcatchers live in coastal sage scrub less than 228m asl (above sea level) in patches greater than 10 hectares. They have been shown to be sensitive to roads, and will not nest in areas with a slope greater than 40%.

California Gnatcatcher San Clemente

Blue-gray Gnatcatcher perched on a branch.

Where are areas of suitable gnatcatcher habitat located?

Summarize Habitat Requirements

Cover type: Coastal sage scrub

Minimum patch size: 10 hectares

Elevation: Less than 228m asl

Excludes areas within 250m and 400m of roads

Obtain Spatial Data

- ☆ Land cover map
- ☆ Road map
- ☆ Digital elevation model (DEM) or triangulated irregular network (TIN) (elevation)

Geoprocessing

The Land Trust team starts with a sketch to plan the sequence of geoprocessing operations necessary to integrate and analyze the data to inform the spatial question. Although it can be tempting not to sketch or diagram your steps first, doing so allows the question to drive the process, not the tools.

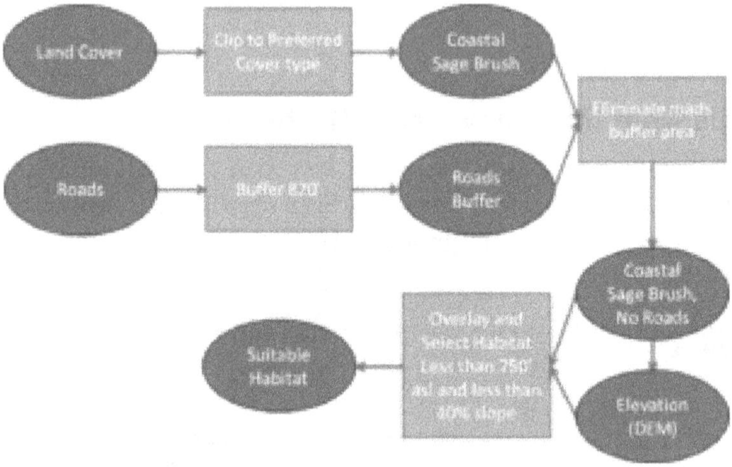

Geoprocessing sketch for gnatcatcher suitable habitat

Then the team uses GIS software to perform the geoprocessing.

Geoprocessing will result in a map showing the location of habitat suitable for gnatcatchers, according to your process.

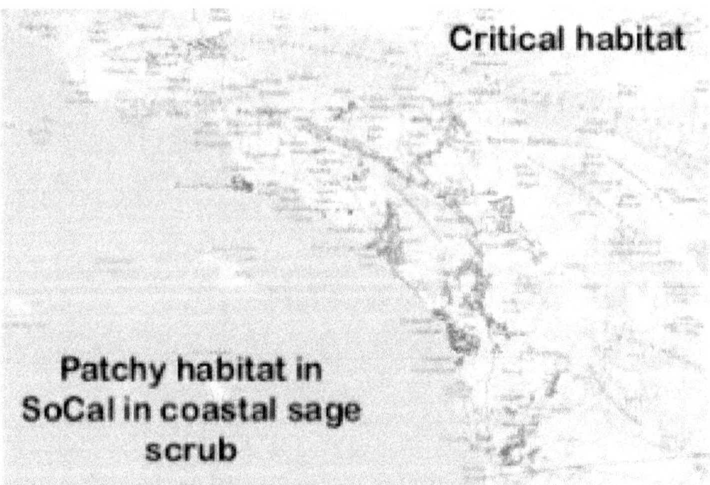

Patchy habitat in southern California for gnatcatcher.

Sensitivity Analysis

Now, what if you are not sure whether your model best represents actual gnatcatcher habitat. Several parameters could be explored to test the sensitivity of the model, including:

☆ **Reducing max permissible slope** from 40% to 30%, 25%, and even 20%. Is most of the available habitat lost when areas with a slope between 40% and

30% are eliminated? How does this affect the decision to protect specific areas?

- ☆ **Increase or decrease buffer around roads or use a more detailed road layer.** Does a larger or smaller buffer or greater number of roads dramatically influence the total habitat area?
- ☆ **Include cat population density.** Do areas of suitable habitat coincide with areas of high cat population density? How does this influence the choice of specific areas?

British shorthair cat hunting birds and mice outside the garden.

3. USING MODELBUILDER

Now let us get our hands dirty and learn how to apply geoprocessing within GIS by opening the toolbox . . .

Geoprocessing operations in GIS are carried out using a set of tools, organized into toolsets, each of which performs a single operation.

- ☆ Data Extraction
- ☆ Overlay
- ☆ Proximity

Data Extraction

There are several methods available to reduce or extract data from larger, more complex datasets to create a new subset of data with just the information needed.

Selection tools—allow you to select features that meet some criteria or that are located in a particular place, or a combination of both, such as "all the non-vacant parcels adjacent to the parkway" (below).

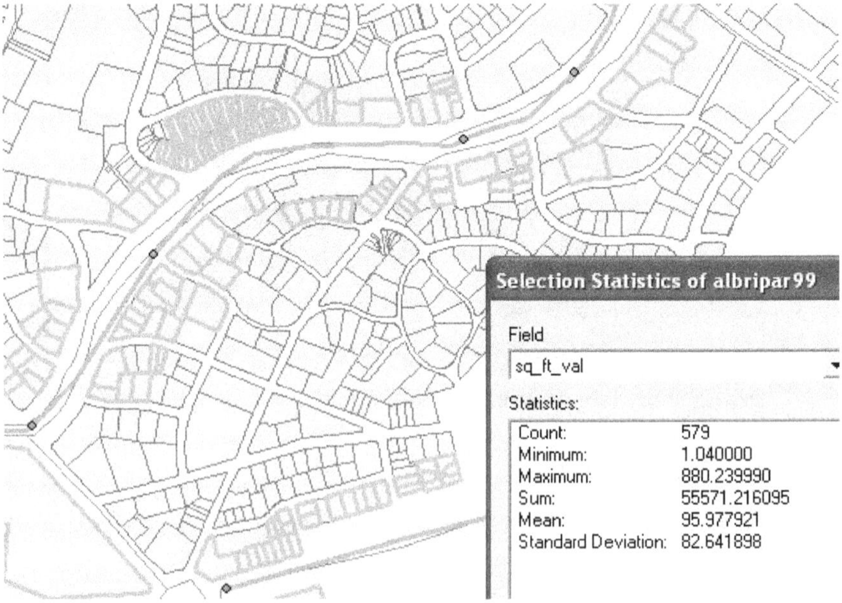

Screen shot of selection statistics from ArcMap

Other basic spatially defined selection tools include the following:

- ☆ **Clipping**—works like a cookie cutter to cut out features from the input layer that fall within the polygons in the clip feature
- ☆ **Splitting**—creates multiple output layers from a single feature layer based on polygons or zones of the split features
- ☆ **Dissolving**—combines polygons that share an attribute value into larger polygons, essentially dissolving the border between the features
- ☆ **Eliminating**—combines selected polygons with adjacent polygons that have the largest area or longest shared border. Eliminate is often used to clean up spatial data after digitizing or overlaying features by eliminating sliver polygons

Dissolving and *eliminating* features can be used to extract features that share particular attributes, and combine them into larger features with less diversity

Dissolve

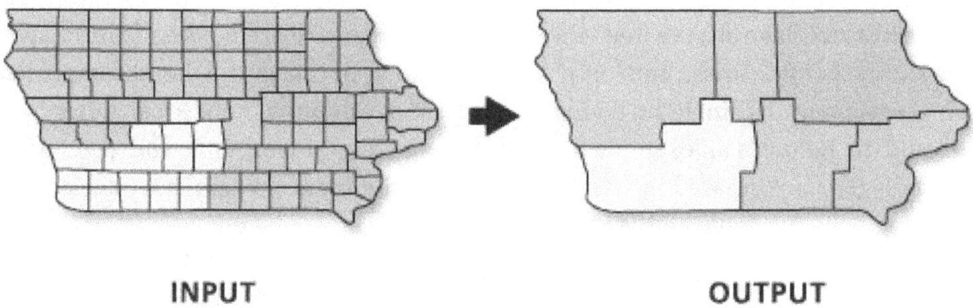

Eliminate

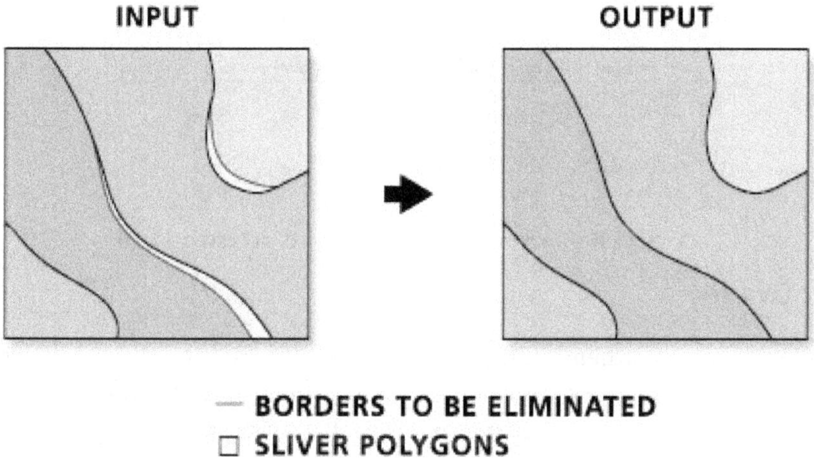

Images from Esri resource center

Overlay

Spatial Overlay

Spatial overlay superimposes multiple datasets with a common coordinate system, resulting in a new dataset that identifies the spatial relationships between multiple data layers.

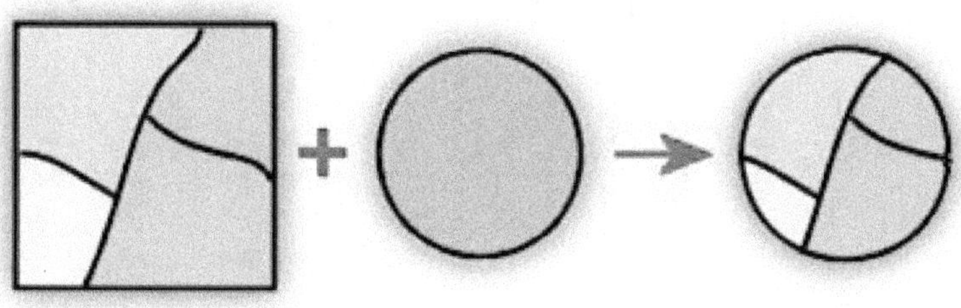

Vector Overlays

Vector overlays are created when a polygon layer is placed over a feature layer containing points, lines, and/or polygons. Vector overlays can be accomplished using several tools, including identity, intersect, union, symmetrical difference, and update. Below is an example of an overlay of steep slopes, soils, and vegetation. New polygons are created by the intersection of the input polygon boundaries. The resulting polygons have all the attributes of the original polygons.

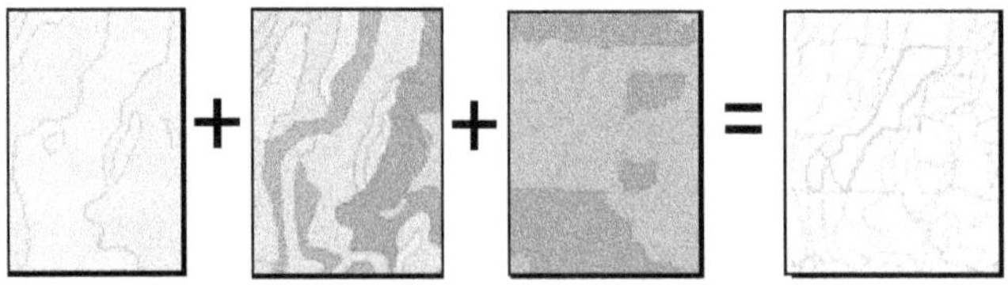

FID	Shape*	FID_soils	CODE	CLASS	FID_sl	SLOPE	FID_veg	DET_TYPE
3039	Polygon	508	38F	6	0	60	117	A
3040	Polygon	508	38F	6	0	60	119	SS
3041	Polygon	508	38F	6	0	60	157	U
3042	Polygon	508	38F	6	0	60	158	A
3043	Polygon	508	38F	6	0	60	160	FC

ArcGIS Resources Center, Desktop 10, accessed 12.16

Raster Overlay

Raster overlay mathematically merges two or more sets of data that share a common grid to create a new set of values for a single output layer. Raster overlay tools include combine, zonal statistics, map algebra, weighted overlay, and weighted sum. Below is an example of raster overlay by addition for suitability modeling. Three raster layers (steep slopes, soils, and vegetation) are ranked for development suitability on a scale of 1–7. When the layers are added (bottom), each cell is ranked on a scale of 3–21.

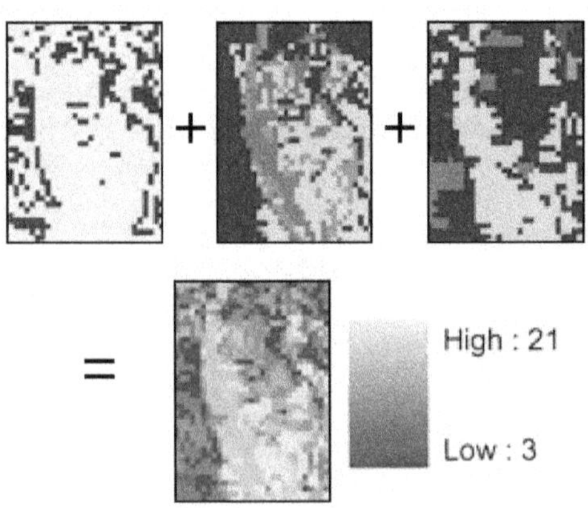

ArcGIS Resource Center, Desktop 10, accessed 12.16

Proximity

Proximity tools find the distance of cells or proximity of features to one another and operate differently depending on the input data model.

Vector Proximity Tools

Vector proximity tools include buffer, near, point distance, select by location, and others. The images below illustrate a line (left) and point (right) buffer.

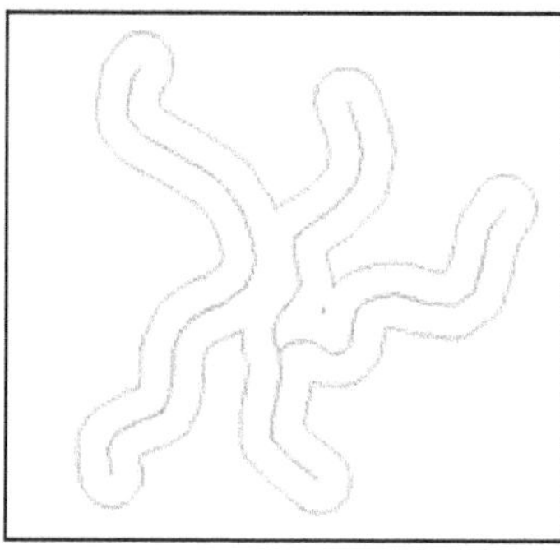
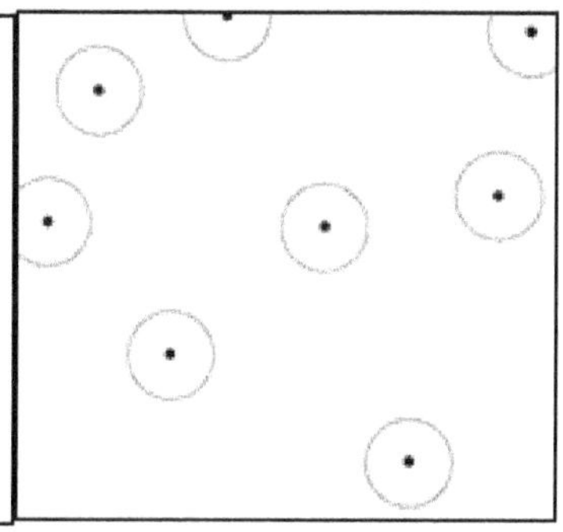

Raster Distance Tools

Raster distance tools include Euclidean distance, Euclidean direction, cost distance, cost allocation, and others. The image below illustrates output of the Euclidean Distance tool, where the value of each cell is the distance to the nearest river feature.

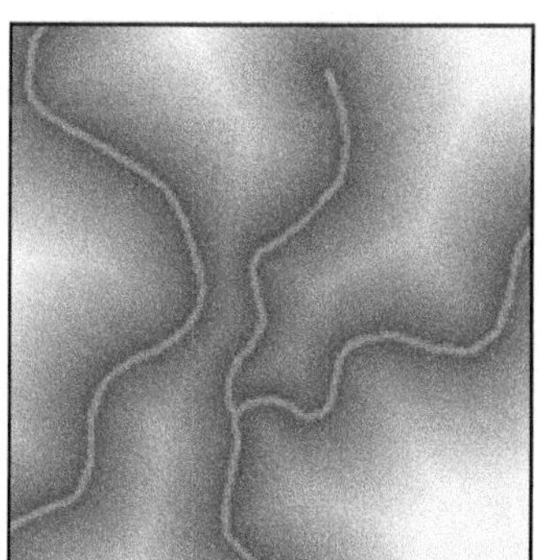

Using Model Builder

There are several ways to spatially select portions of a data layer.

Set Algebra

Remember learning what fit in a set in elementary algebra? Set algebra chooses areas with attributes that are >, <, or = to some specified criteria.

For example, you could select all areas that are not "New York" (upper right), or all counties that are at least 1000 square miles in area (lower left):

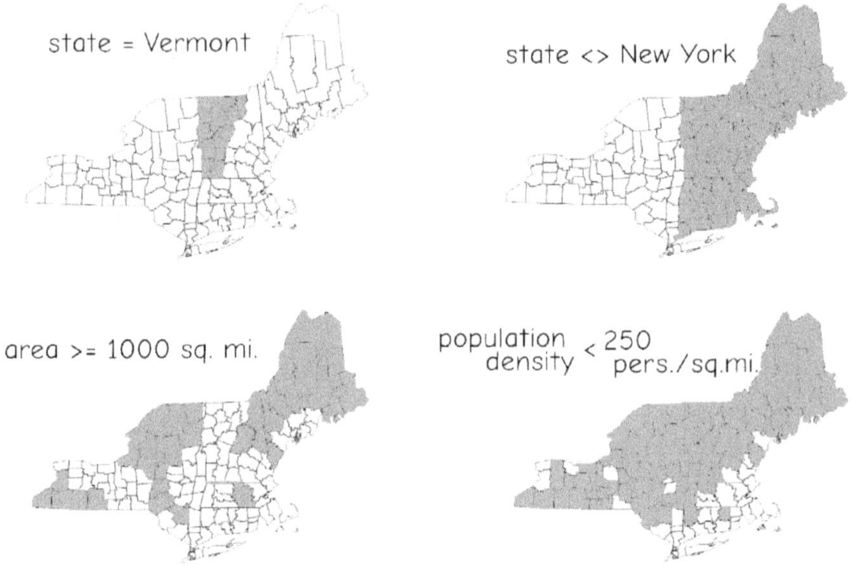

Counties in the northeastern US selected with set algebra. From Bolstad 2016 fig. 9-6, recolored for illustration

Boolean Operations

Similar to Set Algebra, Boolean algebra chooses areas with attributes matching specified criteria using AND, OR, NOT operations.

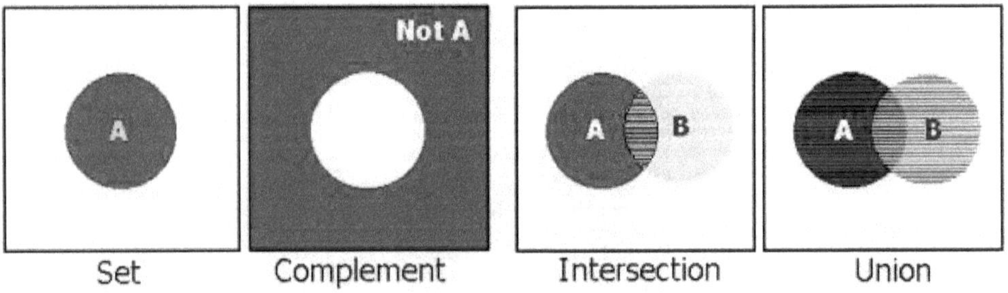

Intelligent Solutions Inc., accessed 12.16

Fuzzy Set

Fuzzy selection is less commonly used in GIS than other selection sets. When attribute data are imprecise or inaccurate, fuzzy logic can be used to define how **likely** it is that a particular feature or cell is a member of a set. In the example below, fuzzy sets are used to identify the likelihood that an individual will fall into the "tall" class. You might also imagine this applied to environmental features, like the probability that energy sites will have high radon levels. We will come back to fuzzy logic more later.

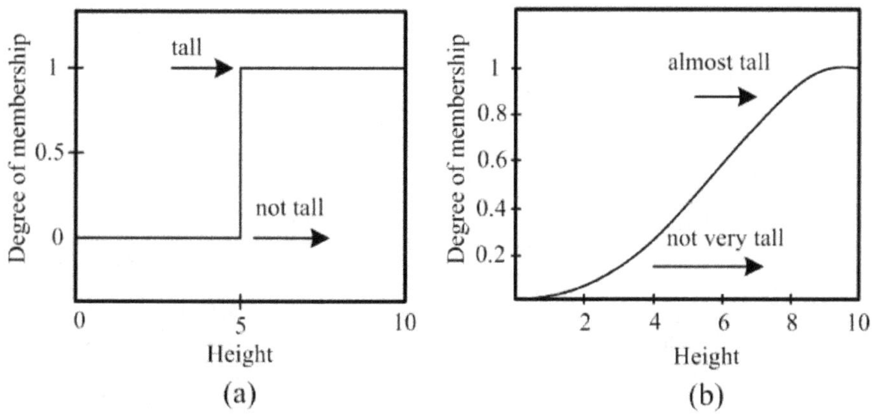

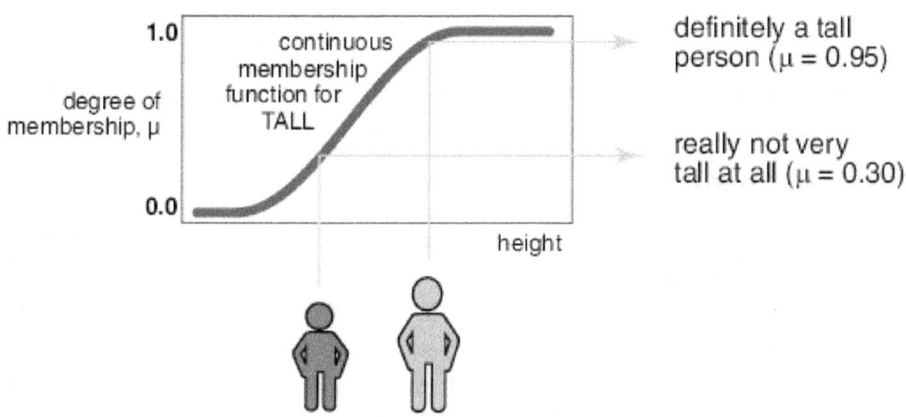

Moradlou et al. 2013

Geoprocess Functions

Geoprocessing tools can be linked together to perform a series of operations necessary to produce the output that answers a spatial question. Each step produces intermediate output on which the next operation acts.

In the example below, buffers are created around the lakes and roads in their respective layers and then overlaid to eliminate areas where roads intersect lake buffers. The hydric status layer is recoded to identify wetlands. Then the wetlands layer and combined buffers layer are overlaid, and areas where the lake buffer and wetland buffer coincide are recoded with a suitability ranking.

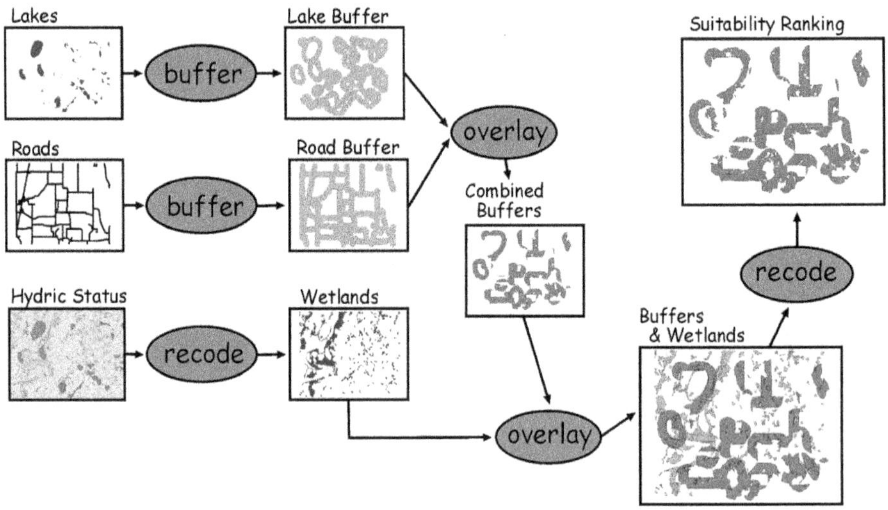

Example of linked geoprocessing steps. Figure from Bolstad 2016, recolored for illustration here.

Geoprocess Demo

In ArcGIS, geoprocessing tools are accessible from ArcToolbox and ArcCatalog and are stored in toolsets, which are stored in toolboxes. Please click here to watch a YouTube demonstration of the use of ArcToolbox in ArcMap 10. The video is approximately 11 minutes long.

Here you see how geoprocessing tools are organized in ArcToolbox of ArcGIS (left) and the Geoalgorithms Toolbox in QGIS (right):

<table>
<tr>
<td>
</td>
<td>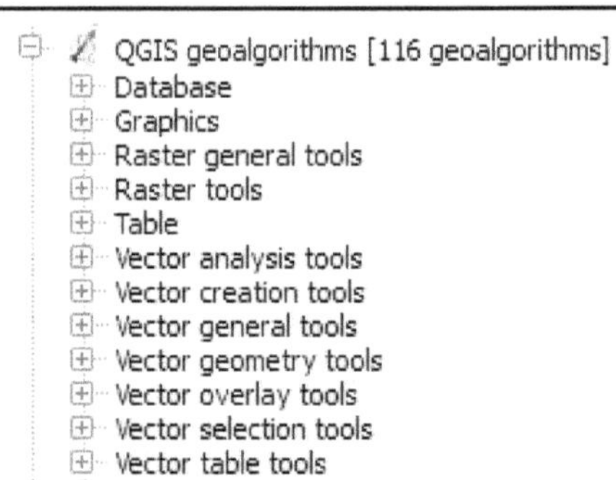
</td>
</tr>
<tr>
<td>Toolsets within ArcToolbox</td>
<td>Geoalgorithms within QGIS processing menu. Screenshot from QGIS. Data from Natural Earth.</td>
</tr>
</table>

Below shows a geoprocessing tool pop-up window accessed from the toolbar on the right in QGIS:

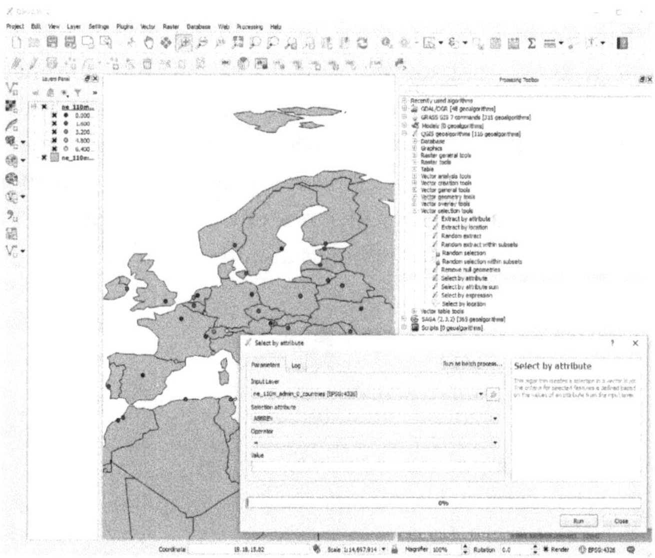

Screenshot from QGIS. Data from Natural Earth.

Geoprocess Model Design

Geoprocessing sequences are also referred to as a "model." Consider these typical steps in designing your first **geoprocessing model**:

- ☆ Determine which geoprocessing tools you need (based on your spatial question).
- ☆ Have your spatial data prepared and organized in Catalog.
- ☆ Determine the order in which the geoprocessing tools should be used.
- ☆ Locate the first tool and open its dialog box.
- ☆ Enter the tool parameters, including the input and output datasets.
- ☆ Run the tool.
- ☆ Repeat steps 3–5 for each geoprocessing tool. Rearrange as needed.
- ☆ Examine the final output and repeat some or all of the analysis steps as needed.

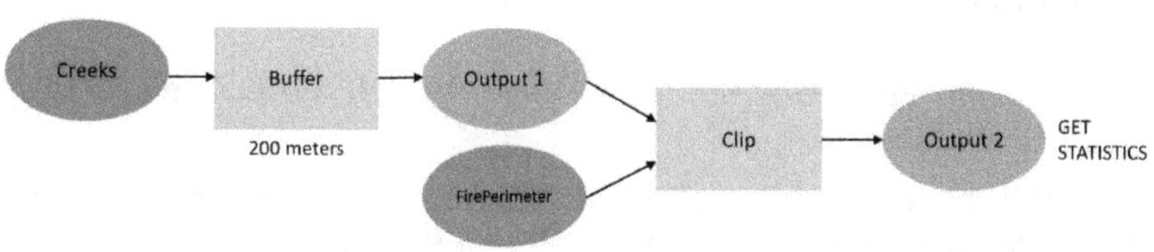

Geoprocess model example from Bolstad, recolored here for illustration.

Model Builder

A model is a collection of geoprocessing operations that automatically execute in sequence when the model is run to produce a final output dataset. These can be put together using **ModelBuilder in ArcGIS, or Graphical Modeler in QGIS**. Any geoprocessing operation in a model can be modified, and then the model can be run again to quickly refine an analysis or produce new data that support an alternative ("what if?") scenario. Geoprocessing models are often used . . .

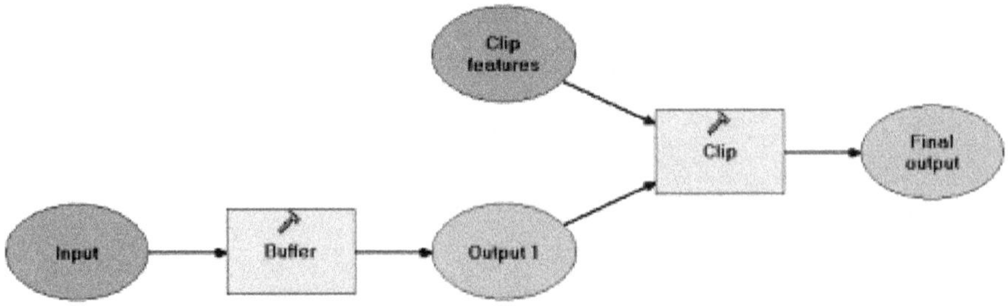

- ☆ For linking and automating analyses
- ☆ To document the flow through the processes of a project
- ☆ To modify inputs and processes easily in a graphic environment (e.g., to run a sensitivity analysis)
- ☆ To automate a repetitive process (e.g., multiple scenarios) to save time and effort.

For more, see this page on ArcGIS Desktop Analytics.

http://www.qgistutorials.com/en/docs/processing_graphical_modeler.html

Link to QGIS documentation on the graphical modeler: https://docs.qgis.org/2.18/en/docs/user_manual/processing/modeler.html?highlight=graphical%20modeler

Topic 3 Knowledge Check

Please answer the following questions to complete Lesson 3 (**note:** click the + sign to enlarge graphics).

REFERENCES

Bolstad, Paul. 2016. GIS Fundamentals. 5th ed. XanEdu Press, http://www.paulbolstad.net/gisbook.html

Kerski, Joseph J. and Jill Clark. 2012. The GIS Guide to Public Domain Data. Esri Press, Redlands, CA 372 pp. Chapter 7 accompanies this lesson.

Moradlou, Majid, Farzaneh Eshaghian Dorcheh, and Mehdi Bigdeli. 2013. "Application of Superposition and Fuzzy Logic Methods to Determine the Contribution of the Utility and Customer in Creation of Harmonic Distortions in PCC Bus." International Journal of Energy Engineering 3 (3): 138–46.

CHAPTER-4

ACCESSING PUBLIC ENVIRONMENTAL DATA THROUGH PARTNERSHIPS AND MAPPING GREEN INFRASTRUCTURE

In this lesson, you will:

- ☆ Integrate public environmental spatial data available through partnerships
- ☆ Learn to use spatial optimization strategies and performance dashboards to evaluate options
- ☆ Apply public environmental data to map green infrastructure
- ☆ Review methods to make good maps

Lesson 4 Topics

This lesson covers three topics. We recommend working through each topic in the order in which they are listed below.

- ☆ Public environmental spatial data and partnerships
- ☆ Spatial Optimization Strategies and Performance
- ☆ Applying Data and Strategies to Green Infrastructure
- ☆ Review Cartography Best Practices

1. PUBLIC ENVIRONMENTAL SPATIAL DATA AND PARTNERSHIPS

Emerging geographic information system themes and directions

Since its inception, geographic information system (GIS) data and tools have developed at a rapid pace. According to Kerski and Clark (2012, Chapter 10), the future of GIS will develop along at least four fronts:

- ☆ New spatial data
- ☆ New partnerships
- ☆ New methods and tools
- ☆ New platforms

In this topic, we focus on new environmental spatial data and partnerships. Topics 2 and 3 address the other two fronts: new methods, tools, and platforms.

As you've seen, **environmental spatial data** are available in the public domain—from established mapping and land management organizations as well as organizations that have not previously been the providers of geographic data.

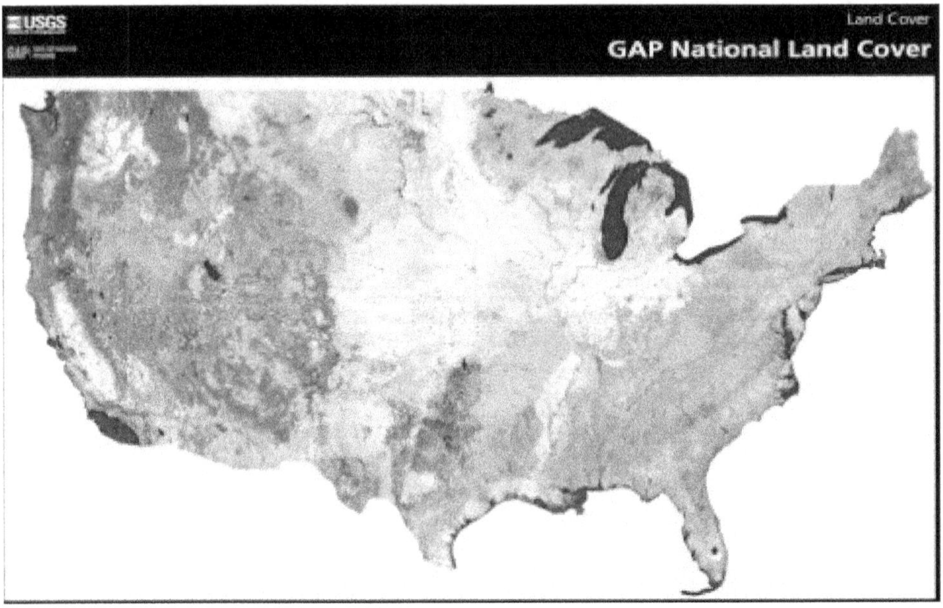

gapanalysis.usgs.gov/gaplandcover/, accessed 12.16

For example, The Nature Conservancy (TNC) provides map services via TNCMaps, an online data portal for vector data related to its conservation initiatives and land holdings that can be accessed as shapefiles or geodatabase formats using standard GIS platforms.

State and federal governments also release data, such as the seamless national land cover vegetation raster dataset that represents the culmination of the Gap Analysis Program (GAP) and was made available through a collaborative effort between the United States Geological Survey (USGS) and the University of Idaho. GAP collects and distributes data to answer the fundamental question, "How well are we protecting common plants and animals?" by identifying those species and plant communities that are not adequately represented in existing conservation lands. To do so, a Gap analysis identifies species' habitat and distribution, protected lands in relation to those species, and where there is a "gap" in protection for species. GAP raster and vector data are used widely across the United States for conservation planning. You will have a chance to work with GAP later.

The LANDFIRE project represents another collaborative effort between government agencies (US Forest Service and US Department of the Interior) and nonprofits (TNC) to produce over 20 national geospatial data layers in raster, vector, and tabular formats, including vegetation, fuel, and disturbances among many others. LandFire is not just for fire! While early on it was a response to large wildland fires and their mitigation and impact, LandFire is used more broadly now for a variety of land change assessments.

Meanwhile, high-resolution imagery and three-dimensional (3D) data are more widely available and accessible to environmental applications through public domain sources. Perhaps the fastest growing demand from environmental applications is for Light Detection and Ranging (LIDAR) data.

LIDAR is a remote sensing method that uses pulses of light energy to generate 3D data of the structure of the earth's surface. The data can be collected from a variety of platforms, including satellites, airplanes, and ground-based devices.

Many agencies are collecting LIDAR to generate data for different applications, including national elevation models for sea-level rise impact studies, data on the structure of vegetation in natural areas to estimate ecosystem productivity and habitat quality, and urban infrastructure for storm water management and flooding scenarios. Here is a link to free lidar data sources: http://gisgeography.com/top-6-free-lidar-data-sources/

LIDAR data are often collected by air, such as with this NOAA survey aircraft (right) over Bixby Bridge in Big Sur, Calif. Here, LIDAR data reveal a top-down (top left) and profile view of Bixby Bridge. NOAA scientists use LIDAR-generated products to examine both natural and man-made environments. LIDAR data support activities such as inundation and storm surge modeling, hydrodynamic modeling, shoreline mapping, emergency response, hydrographic surveying, and coastal vulnerability analysis. (https://oceanservice.noaa.gov/facts/lidar.html).

In many cases, LIDAR or other high-resolution imagery is acquired independently for specific applications, where the sensor is contracted to be flown over a certain area and time. However, LIDAR datasets for many coastal areas can be downloaded from the Office for Coastal Management Digital Coast web portal.

As GAP, LANDFIRE, and LIDAR data illustrate, **partnerships** have forged that enable increased access to and sharing of geospatial data by the general public.

In turn, tools for accessing this data have become more user-friendly as a result of government–private partnerships, which led to the development of Data.gov, for example, collaboration between ESRI and government agencies.

Even as access to data and online visualization tools are readily available, more and more tools continue to enable analysis of environmental spatial data via the web.

Cloud Computing

Cloud computing enables remote, network access to a shared pool of resources. The cloud consists of networks, servers, data storage, applications, and services. In GIS, cloud computing enables users to access data and run software remotely, access services and clients, and host content.

Cloud-based mapping programs like ArcGIS.com facilitate access to publicly available spatial data and mapping, especially for those without access to or training in desktop GIS.

Data Basin

Likewise, several organizations have online data portals with the added functionality of data sharing, discussion boards, and groups that enable data portals to become **intellectual communities.** DataBasin, hosted by the Conservation Biology Institute, is an example of such an online community that you learned about earlier.

https://databasin.org/, accessed 12.16

Sea Sketch

Similarly, SeaSketch is an online tool developed by the McClintock Lab in the Marine Science Institute at the University of California Santa Barbara to enable collaborative planning for ocean conservation.

SeaSketch allows users to generate information—they can produce and share sketches, edit and share views of maps, discuss their ideas, and post sketches to larger discussion forums. This allows users to participate in marine spatial planning without the need for GIS training or software.

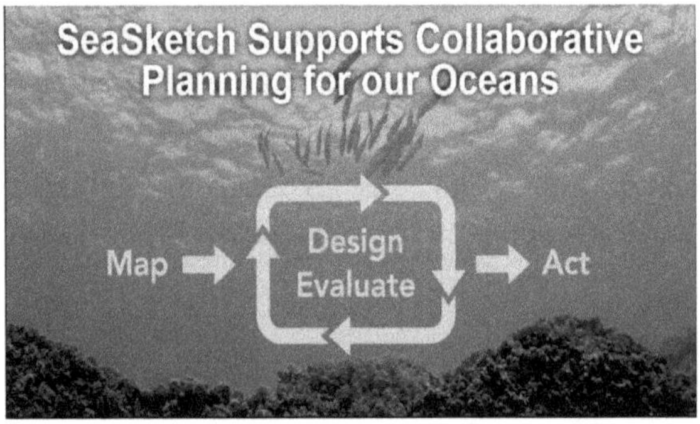

Nature Serve

Nature Serve represents another kind environmental partnership—a network of over 80 programs (e.g., state natural heritage) and scientists serving spatial data and solutions for biodiversity protection. Nature Serve has a page of data, maps, and tools to support a variety of land management assessments and stewardship.

Ecological Land Units Map and Data Sets of World

Another great example of new spatial data and new partnerships in a cloud computing environment is the **Ecological Land Units Map and Data Sets of World.** This Esri Insider post and Storymap describe the Global Ecological Land Units for an analysis.

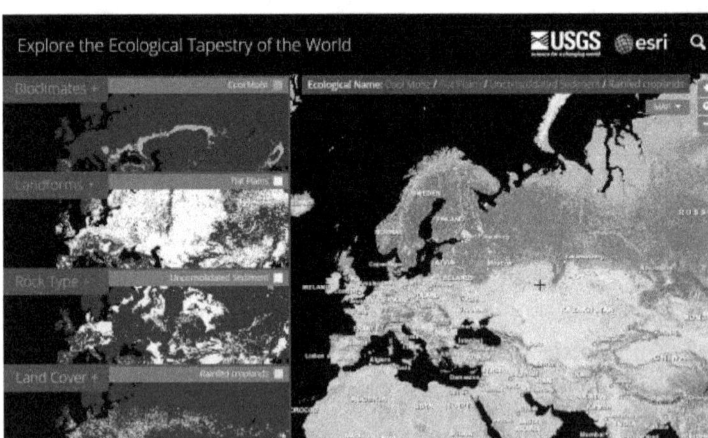

Finally, we conclude this topic with Kerski's top 10 list of useful geospatial data portals (from January 2017)

https://spatialreserves.wordpress.com/2017/01/29/a-top-10-list-of-useful-geospatial-data-portals/

Topic 1 Knowledge Check

Please answer the following questions to proceed to the next topic.

2. SPATIAL OPTIMIZATION STRATEGIES: SUITABILITY AND VULNERABILITY ANALYSES WITH OVERLAY

Last week you learned how to ask spatial questions, select the appropriate geoprocessing steps, and string them together with Model Builder. Here we build on those skills with more complex spatial design and decision-based questions.

Spatial Optimization Strategies

Suitability and vulnerability analyses are sometimes referred to as **spatial optimization strategies** because both attempt to optimize the best (or worst) locations for a given land use.

Suitability

With suitability, we might be optimizing siting for a new housing development or habitat for wolves.

Suitability analyses tend to be:

- ☆ Offensive, or proactive
- ☆ Development oriented
- ☆ Ask "What places are best for . . ."
- ☆ Location optimal

Finding the best route to connect two segments of the Ice Age Trail is an example of a suitability optimization.

Vulnerability

With vulnerability, we often seek to find areas that are most at-risk from a proposed land use.

Vulnerability analyses tend to be:

- ☆ Defensive
- ☆ Conservation or protection oriented
- ☆ Ask "What places are worst for or will be most impacted by . . . ?" or "Where are the greatest risks?"

☆ Location sensitive

Identifying the areas potentially impacted by proposed Penokee-Gogebic mine in Northern Wisconsin is an example of an optimization strategy aimed at vulnerability assessment.

Overlay Analysis

GIS is often used to tackle one of the most foundational spatial optimization questions: What's on top of what, or where do features overlap on the ground? **Overlay tools** simply combine different layers of spatial data, building on Boolean logic you learned earlier.

The Overlay toolset contains tools to overlay multiple feature classes to combine spatial features through map algebra, resulting in a new feature class. New information is created when overlaying one set of features with another.

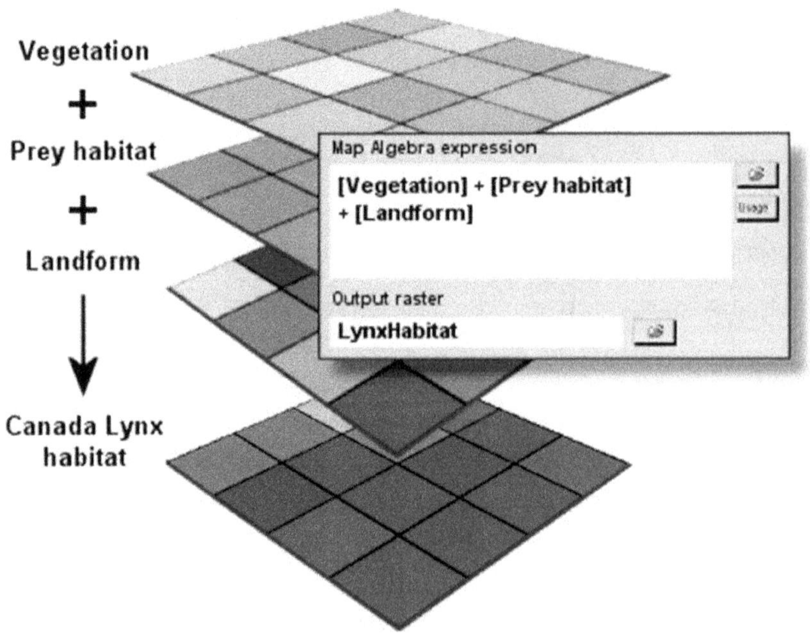

Overlay of vegetation, prey habitat, and landform to identify Canada Lynx habitat.
Source: Esri

This example shows how vegetation, prey habitat, and landform can be combined by raster addition. The resulting composite map or overlay identifies areas that are most likely to provide Canada Lynx habitat.

When you wish to overlay the layers with differing amounts of influence, they can be weighted based on their importance to produce a weighted overlay in GIS.

You saw a sample of weighted overlay in our geoprocessing topic. A **weighted overlay** tool is a specialized overlay analysis to solve multicriteria problems with variable weights, such as site selection suitability and vulnerability analyses.

Geoprocessing for Overlay Analysis

Behind the scenes of any complex overlay analysis is some kind of geoprocessing sequence. The geoprocessing model below was built for the City of Asheville, North Carolina, to identify "priority places" for new business development. The model included a series of input layers like roads, parks, and business centers that could be selected by attributes or location, and each could be weighted differently.

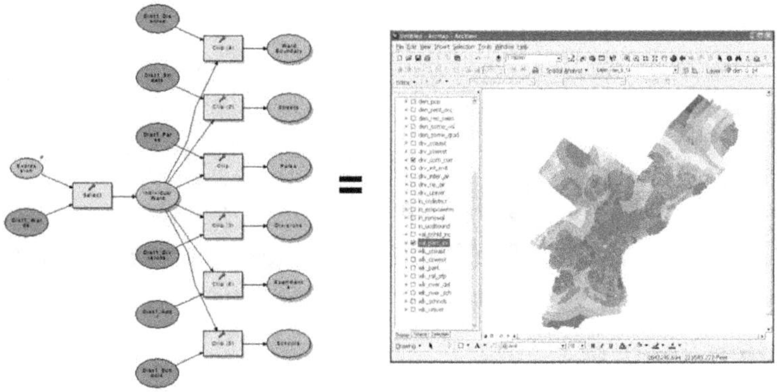

Priority Places weighted overlay, https://www.azavea.com/projects/priority-places/

The Priority Places tool used **weighted overlay** to choose the location of a new business in the City of Asheville.

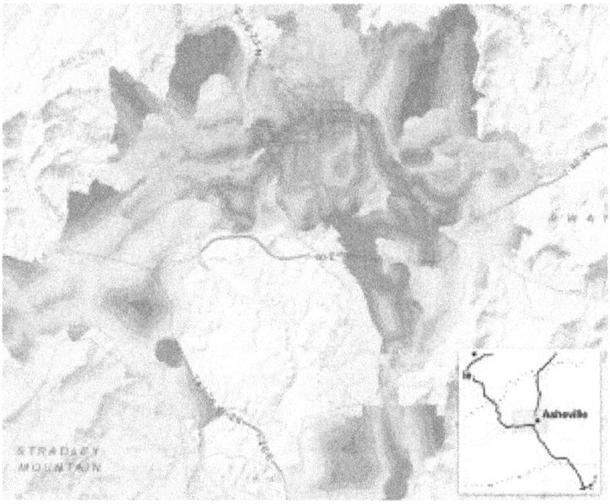

Priority Places sample overlay output

Citizens and decision-makers of Asheville, however, did not see the weighted overlay model running in the background. Instead, they interfaced with an interactive user dashboard where they selected the input layers, criteria (e.g., distance from), and weights to identify their priority places.

Priority Places interactive suitability analysis tool

Automating Geoprocessing

To run more complex alternative scenarios, there are mechanisms for automating geoprocessing.

For example, in the ArcGIS ModelBuilder application, the following tools are used to automate the process of using different inputs or criteria and generating a variety of outputs:

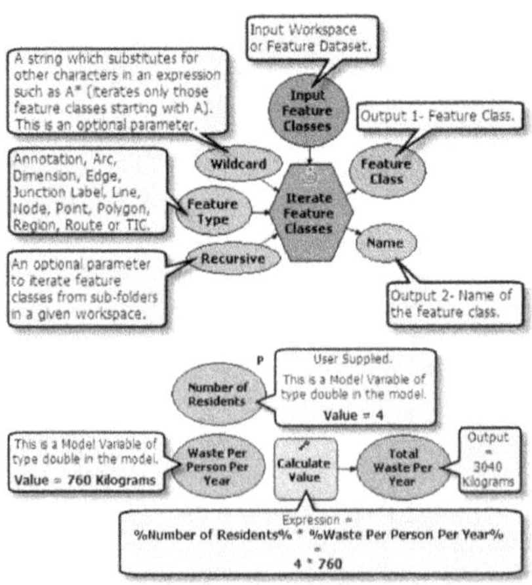

Automating tools for ArcGIS Model Builder. ArcGIS Resource Center, accessed 12.15

- ☆ In-line variable substitution
- ☆ Lists
- ☆ Iteration
- ☆ Feedback

Learning to use these functions is beyond the scope of this book. However, if you are interested in learning more on your own, visit Advanced Techniques in ModelBuilder.

ModelBuilder provides a graphical interface for generating a model that can automatically run a geoprocessing sequence with different inputs and criteria. On the back end, the computer is running code to execute the model you created visually. For example, many GIS programs use the programming language, Python. In some cases, it may be more efficient or allow more flexibility to script a model by writing lines of Python code than by building a graphical model. ArcGIS and QGIS allow users to view and edit the Python code generated by their model building tools, though it's always good to start any model or scripting by drawing out what you want to do first!

Performing Sensitivity Analysis

Sensitivity analysis is used to explore how the output of spatial optimization strategies—suitability and vulnerability analysis—change with slight variations in the input criteria parameters.

For example, in a housing suitability model to identify the most desired locations to add building lots based on specified criteria—slope, aspect, distance to river—sensitivity analysis could be performed by changing each of the input criteria by small increments and measuring the resulting changes in output. For example, does a 50-m increase in distance from the river dramatically decrease the area suitable for housing?

A model, whether built graphically with model building tools or through scripting in a programming language, enables users to quickly perform sensitivity analyses by changing these parameters in a suitability or vulnerability model. Using lists, series, or reclassification tables can facilitate iterations of models for efficiently running sensitivity analyses.

Topic 2 Knowledge Check

Please answer the following questions to proceed to the next topic.

3. APPLYING ENVIRONMENTAL SPATIAL DATA AND PARTNERSHIPS TO MAP AND ASSESS GREEN INFRASTRUCTURE

Next we apply public environmental spatial data and partnerships to spatial optimization applications with **green infrastructure**.

Grey Infrastructure

Think of all the hard facilities and structures that connect and run the machine of our built environment (roads, storm drains, sewers, culverts, etc.). We call that necessary network "grey infrastructure."

A likely combined sewer overflow outlet in Bayonne, NJ	**Melted water flows down through the manhole**

Green Infrastructure

Equally important is the network of streams, wetlands, greenways, green roofs, and natural corridors, called "green infrastructure," for absorbing rainwater, filtering storm water, holding slopes from erosion, reducing urban heat, and connecting habitats. Worldwide, the need to identify, design, and maintain green infrastructure networks takes a priority seat next to grey infrastructure for communities and regional planners. To facilitate planning for green infrastructure, especially across boundaries, partnerships like the World Green Infrastructure Network and Green Infrastructure Collaborative of US agencies take the helm.

WORLD GREEN INFRASTRUCTURE NETWORK vegetation makes it possible!	Green Infrastructure Collaborative
http://www.worldgreenroof.org/index.html	*https://www.epa.gov/green-infrastructure/green-infrastructure-collaborative*

Since 2014, the US EPA (Environmental Protection Agency) coalesced other federal agencies, nongovernmental organizations, and private sector entities into the *Green Infrastructure Collaborative, "a network-based learning alliance created to help communities more easily implement green infrastructure."* Depending on their focus, different organizations, networks or agencies emphasize and define green infrastructure differently. For instance, the EPA's focus for green infrastructure is primarily on storm water.

Their definition reads: Green infrastructure is a cost-effective, resilient approach to managing wet weather impacts that provides many community benefits. While single-purpose gray storm water infrastructure—conventional piped drainage and water treatment systems—is designed to move urban storm water away from the built environment, green infrastructure reduces and treats storm water at its source while delivering environmental, social, and economic benefits.

Residential building in the public green park during sunrise.

Alternatively, the World Green Infrastructure Network (WGIN) focuses on growing the network of green roofs and walls:

The World Green roof Infrastructure Network collects and disseminates knowledge, information and data concerning roof and wall greening, worldwide.

FUKUOKA, JAPAN—JUL 09: View of Acros Fukuoka on Jul 09, 2015, in Fukuoka, Japan. Across Fukuoka is the eco-building and landmark of Fukuoka that has a green roof.

Others approach green infrastructure from protected areas management and conservation. Identifying our most valuable places to protect for future generations begins with spatial optimization—essentially broad-scale suitability and vulnerability analyses. Here, green infrastructure is applied as a spatial concept to understand the best places for growth and choose development that has smaller footprints, protects key habitats, and makes landscapes more connected and resilient. In this case, natural resources are seen as part of connected infrastructure that supports our everyday lives.

This view drove Esri founder and president to launch a Green Infrastructure Initiative, *"to assemble, evaluate, and produce a model to enable governments to protect and restore biodiversity while guiding economic development decisions."*

—Jack Dangermond, Esri.com/greeninfrastructure

Esri's initiative defines green infrastructure as:

". . . a strategically planned and managed network of open space, watersheds, wildlife habitats, parks, and other natural and seminatural areas that enrich and sustain communities."

The green infrastructure initiative provides a system or model, along with tools and spatial data to map green infrastructure. The model is built around several key components to be mapped and overlaid:

- Ecological resources
- Cultural, historic, and scenic resources (including parks and recreation)

- Hazard areas that pose environmental risks or costs
- Connections, or networks of ecological corridors

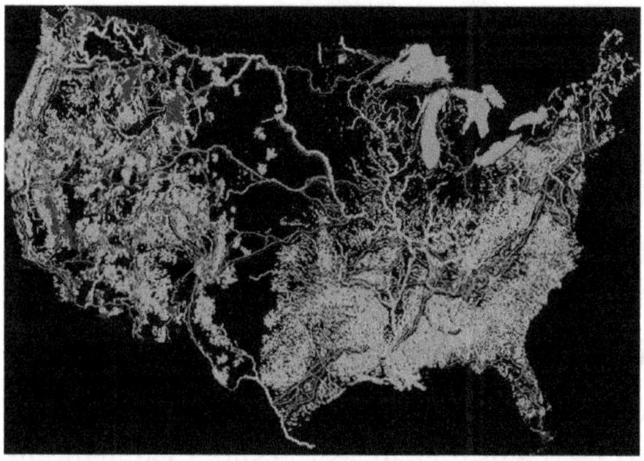

http://www.esri.com/about-esri/greeninfrastructure

At its simplest level, site visitors can enter an address to ask how green their county/town or region is and how green it is likely to be in the future. The web-based green infrastructure mapping tool overlays best available spatial data to determine the amount of intact core habitat and green infrastructure for the selected location relative to the national average.

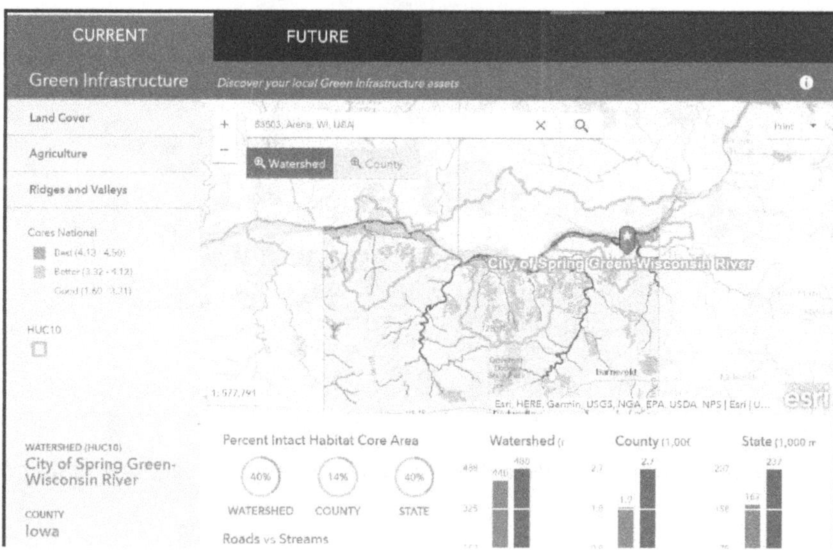

Green Infrastructure mapping tool

There are also a series of advanced apps for green infrastructure analysis and a downloadable ArcToolbox. The apps allow users to select and prioritize landscape cores, rank landscape cores with different weighting scenarios, and conduct a landscape analysis to identify areas with characteristics your community wants to protect. While you might not see it, behind the scenes, the Esri Green Infrastructure apps incorporate many of the tools and data covered in the last few lessons, including:

- ☆ Public environmental spatial data
- ☆ Geoprocessing models for spatial optimization (suitability and vulnerability assessments)
- ☆ Weighted overlay within geoprocessing models
- ☆ Dashboards
- ☆ Scenario management
- ☆ Collaboration and partnerships

For instance, behind the Core Weighting app for green infrastructure, a weighted overlay runs every time the user changes the slider value for any of the spatial data layers in the map. After the weighted overlay is run with new parameters, an updated view of best and better core habitat is displayed.

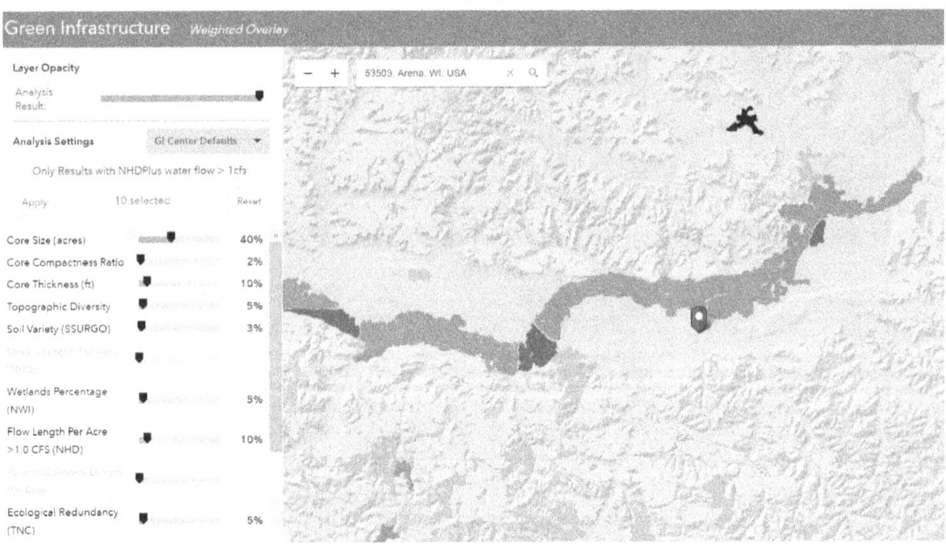

Green Infrastructure dashboard

Here the user interfaces with a dashboard rather than the geoprocessing model.

Dashboards

Dashboards, also called feedback displays, indicate performance metrics of a given alternative spatial designs, such as how many biodiversity cores are in a county or length of a riparian buffer, for example, much like a car dashboard tells how fast you're going and how much fuel is left. When you make changes to the spatial criteria, new performance metrics are displayed.

For example, like Priority Places, the Sustainable Systems Integration Model (SSIM) of Asia Development Bank uses performance dashboards, shown here, to compare alternative design plans against a number of sustainability metrics.

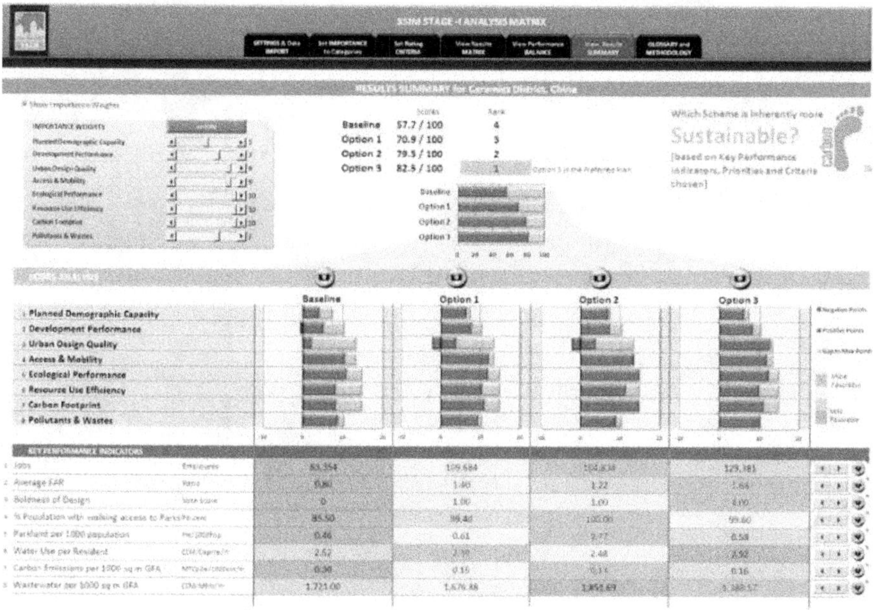

www.scribd.com/document/226085436/Sustainable-System-Integration-Model-SSIM, accessed 12.16

Dashboards are tools to manipulate spatial analyses in an interactive environment with immediate feedback for evaluation. They are especially useful for decision-makers who have little experience with GIS.

Newer and more broadly accessible, the Operations Dashboard for ArcGIS helps users create performance dashboards. As a configurable web app, you can add analytics, metrics, and visualization tools to your web maps through ArcGIS online. The maps and indicators update in real time and can be shared with stakeholders to support collaborative and actionable decision-making.

To read more about this dashboard:

https://www.gis-professional.com/content/news/esri-releases-operations-dashboard-for-arcgis

https://www.esri.com/en-us/arcgis/products/operations-dashboard/overview

Scenario Management

Finally, scenario management can be essential for large green infrastructure or other spatial optimization projects. When examining many alternative options, changing parameters slightly here and there, the number of scenarios multiplies quickly, and it is easy to lose track of which was which. Scenario management tools keep track and help organize scenario outputs.

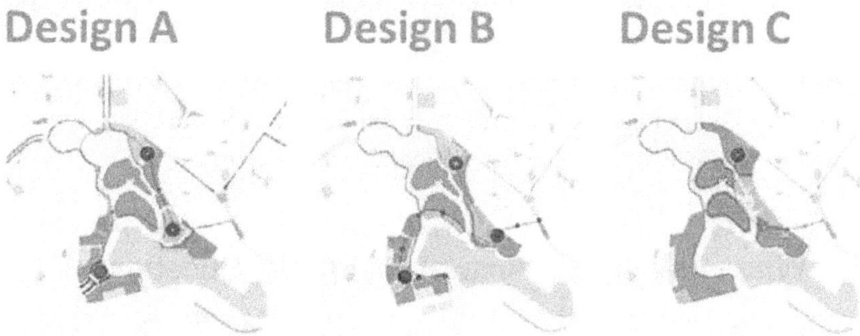

Putting it all together with ArcGIS Pro

If there could be a hybrid of desktop GIS and web mapping, it is ArcGIS Pro. Pro works with existing map documents alongside any of the ArcGIS Desktop applications (e.g., ArcMap, ArcCatalog), with all the robust visualization, geoprocessing, and analytical tools. Then, like GIS online, you can share your map projects through the cloud.

The ArcGIS Pro interface will look similar yet different to ArcMap. It was launched in 2015 and is becoming mainstream.

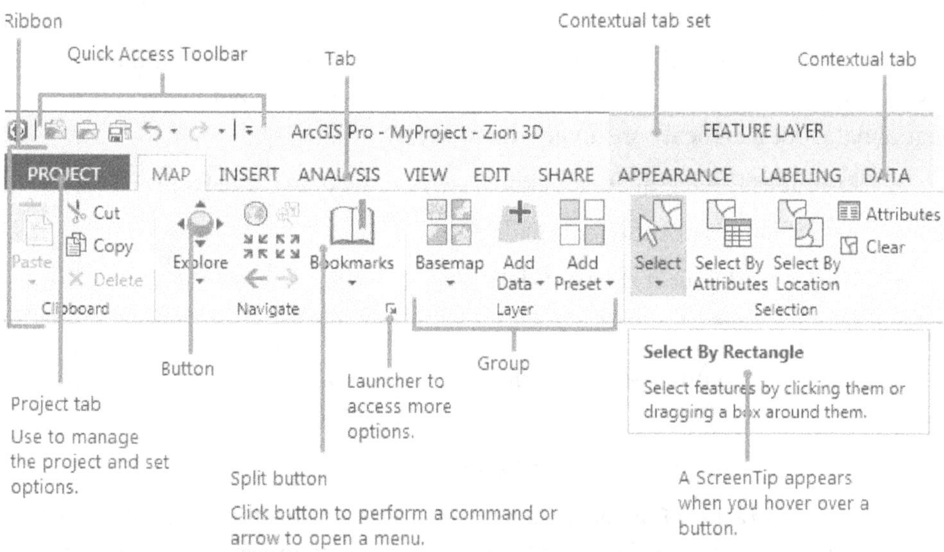

From: pro.arcgis.com/en/pro-app/get-started/overview-of-arcgis-pro.htm, accessed 12.16

Sharing Maps and Collaborating with ArcGIS Pro

Besides its capabilities for working with two-dimensional (2D) and 3D spatial data, imagery, and visualizations, ArcGIS Pro enables collaborative mapping by directly connecting to online web maps and layers. You can author your map with existing web or public data layers, or with your own data layers. You can then share your web map and layers back out to groups or public for collaboration. Web maps can be opened in ArcGIS Pro as well as in standard web browsers.

Learn more about sharing web maps.

Key Points When Asking and Answering Spatial Questions

As we wrap up Lesson 4 and the Collecting and Mapping Data module, let's end with some key points to remember when asking and answering spatial questions.

1. Mind the process

Remember that when engaging in the process of geographic inquiry (or spatial thinking) you should always:

- ☆ Establish the goals of your project early on
- ☆ Focus on the problem or question you wish to solve
- ☆ Only work with data that will help you solve that problem

2. Be a critical consumer

Given the trends and QUANTITY of public environmental spatial data, and the ease of sharing map projects, it's important that you become not just a consumer of spatial data, but a critical consumer who always:

- Examines the metadata and knows where the data came from
- Asks if data is of sufficient quality
- Uses only the most relevant data

References

Kerski, Joseph J., and Jill Clark. 2012. *The GIS Guide to Public Domain Data*. Redlands, CA: Esri Press.

ArcGIS Pro Helps You Get Work Done Faster. 2014. Esri.com, summer.

Esri Releases Operations Dashboard for ArcGIS. 2018. GIS Professional. https://www.gis-professional.com/content/news/esri-releases-operations-dashboard-for-arcgis.

Please answer the following questions to proceed to the next topic.

4. CARTOGRAPHY BEST PRACTICES

It is **vital** that your maps looks good! Why?

Because, a good map can convey a ton of information in a short amount of time and to a very wide audience. But a bad map can confuse and even convey things you never meant to say.

What Makes An OK Map?

All good maps **must** have:

☆ A legend

☆ North Arrow

☆ Title

☆ Scale bar

☆ A brief description of the results, and data sources

But, if I were to make a map that only has the features mentioned above, it would look something like this:

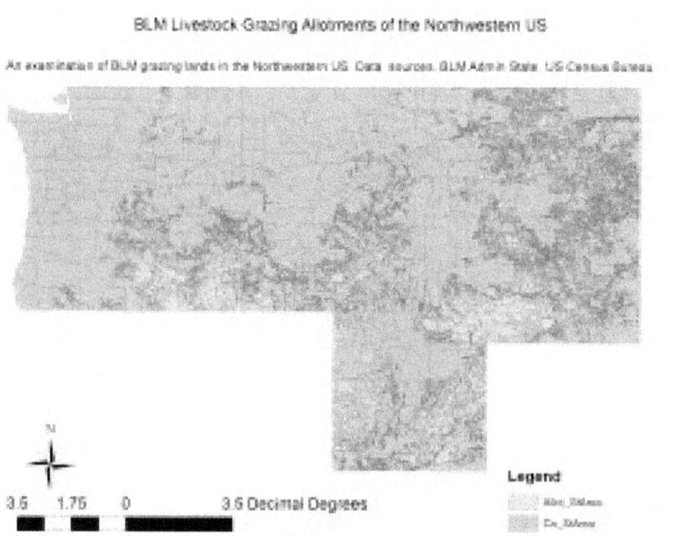

That doesn't look so great. Let's break down why.

☆ The colors aren't great because I haven't put any thought into them, I've let ArcMap make that decision for me, and ArcMap chooses colors randomly.

- ☆ The legend is confusing, the labels have strange names, and if I hadn't made this map they would make no sense to me (they probably make no sense to you!).
- ☆ The title is there, but it could probably be centered better.
- ☆ The north arrow is...actually it's fine.
- ☆ The scale bar is using a really strange scale, making it difficult to understand. ArcMap just defaults to whatever units are being used by ArcMap.
- ☆ I can't really tell what the context of this map is. If I wasn't a US citizen I would have no idea which states these might be.
- ☆ What about the Layers I am using? Is it vital that the counties be included? Might there be a simpler, more intuitive layer to use?

So, the point I am trying to make is that every piece of your map should be designed to help highlight what you are trying to tell the reader. So in this case, I want to highlight the BLM grazing allotment in the Northwestern US. So I will attempt to make this pop by putting the study area into context and using some better colors. Then I will ensure my legend is clear and concise, and I will move things around to make the map aesthetically pleasing . Maps are visual, and so we have to ensure we make them look good!

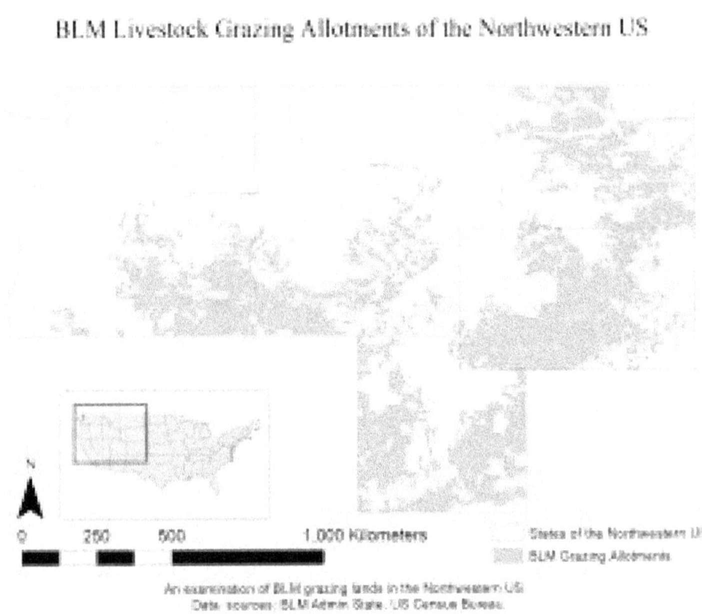

Isn't that better? Why?

- ☆ It's more simple, the colors are cleaner and make the map clearer
- ☆ The map has been put into context, so that it is a but more clear which states are included
- ☆ The scale bar is more clear, and in units that make sense
- ☆ The legend labels make sense

A Note of Colors

Be careful with colors, they can help or hurt you a lot. Make sure you can always tell the difference between colors, and also make sure that you think about your audience. If the map is intended for a very small audience, then the colors can be chosen based more on what you like. But if you are presenting this map to a wider audience, you always have to consider things such as whether or not this map is readable by everyone.

Color Blind Audiences

The most common form of color blindness is red-green color blind, which is most common in men. About 8% of men and 0.4% of women are red-green color blind, which roughly translates to about 1 in 12ss men and 1 in 200 women. Therefore, in any given presentation, the chances are relatively high that someone will be colorblind, meaning that as map makers, we should consider this possibility and create our maps accordingly. That isn't to say that we can never use red or green, but we should be careful about using solely red or solely green scales, and we should always be careful not to use these colors at each end of a scale. Finally, these colors should not be used next to one another. Here are some sources about colors that can used to help find some good color-blind friendly color schemes:

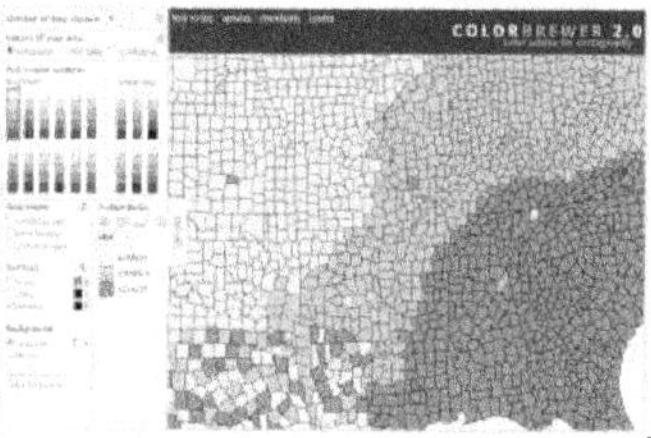

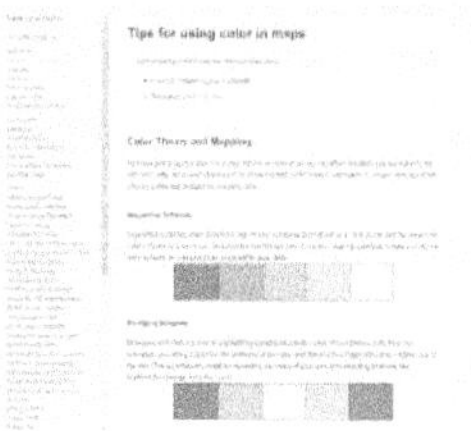

INDEX

www.ingramcontent.com/pod-product-compliance
Lightning Source LLC
Chambersburg PA
CBHW071246230926
51849CB00001B/241
9789390013678